DATE DUE

THE ENGLISH ADVENTURERS

THE ENGLISH ADVENTURERS

by

CLENNELL WILKINSON

Essay Index Reprint Series

BOOKS FOR LIBRARIES PRESS

FREEPORT, NEW YORK

First Published 1931
Reprinted 1968

LIBRARY OF CONGRESS CATALOG CARD NUMBER:
68-26485

PRINTED IN THE UNITED STATES OF AMERICA

. . . I spake of most disastrous chances,
Of moving accidents, by flood and field;
Of hair-breadth 'scapes i' the imminent deadly breach;
Of being taken by the insolent foe,
And sold to slavery . . .
And of the Cannibals that each other eat,
The Anthropophagi, and men whose heads
Do grow beneath their shoulders. . . .
                    Othello, ACT I, Scene iii.

As proper men as ever trod upon neat's leather.
                    Julius Caesar, ACT I, Scene i.

CONTENTS

[*Part of Chapter IV has already appeared in the " London Mercury."
The author is indebted to the editor for permission to reprint.*]

THE
ENGLISH ADVENTURERS

CHAPTER I

WHAT IS AN ADVENTURER?

THE dictionary defines an adventurer as "one
who adventures," and an adventure as "an
accident, a chance, a hazard; an enterprise in which
something is at hazard; a thing or sum sent to sea."
In fact, to engage in an adventure is simply to take
a risk. On that definition I should feel bound to
include in this small volume some record of the
doings of stockbrokers, company promoters and
money-lenders; burglars, gamblers, and those who
provide the money for West-end plays. There is
also the unpleasant significance given to the word
in Victorian times, when "adventurer" meant a
showy-looking man without a bank balance, and
"adventuress" meant a "gold-digger," as we should
call her to-day.

But it is obvious that this vague kind of definition
will not do. I do not pretend to be able to substitute
a better one. But I recognise that when the average
man is told of a book entitled *The English Adventurers*, a clear and precise picture springs to life in
his mind. It is a picture full of colour and romance,

including black-coated missionaries and gaily-dressed buccaneers; heavily armed, sweating Crusaders charging through the desert sands; Elizabethans in their trunk-hose planting the Red Cross of St. George upon the shore of some unknown island in the west; or a few dim, fur-clad figures of modern men staggering through blinding snowstorms towards an ice meadow called the Pole. Every one knows what is meant by the term "adventurer," used in this sense—that is, in the ordinary meaning of the word. But it seems necessary, in order to avoid all risk of misunderstanding, to carry this preliminary explanation just a little further. We leave out speculators in the City, gamblers, highwaymen, and pickpockets—that is agreed. But what about soldiers and sailors in the King's service—not to mention policemen and revenue officers—whose business it is to take frequent "hazards" in the ordinary course of their professions? Are we to include Cromwell, Marlborough, Wellington—adventurous spirits, surely, if the word means anything at all? Or if we take in Anson (as we obviously must), on what excuse can the paladin Nelson be left out?

I find it extraordinarily difficult to explain, though I know that every one will agree with me in making these distinctions. What we are trying to get at is the well understood difference between Sir Robert Knollys and Sir John Chandos. The fact seems to be that if you serve your king for a salary, in however dangerous an employment, and along the ordinary lines of that employment, then you are not an adventurer as the word is used here. But if you are sent off on some sideshow, something out of the ordinary (as Captain Cook was when he explored the South Seas), then you *are*. Or if you go and serve some foreign government in the fighting services, as Cochrane and Gordon did, then again you are. It is all very puzzling. Every great explorer is an adventurer, within the meaning of the act, but every great soldier or sailor is not. Buccaneers and privateers may be included, but naval officers, in the regular exercise of their profession, may not.

Also any adventure in Cochin-China is grist for our mill, but one in the Old Kent Road is not. At the same time we must carefully avoid making this book a mere list of travellers' tales, or a short history of the English explorers.

It comes to this, I think: that there must be real bodily risk attached to every adventure (if there is also a risk of fortune, so much the better, but it is not sufficient in itself); and there must be an element of adventurousness, not only in the actual exploit, but in the undertaking of it. Adventures may crop up in the ordinary course of business, but the man who encounters them, however heroically, has not earned the title of "adventurer" as we mean it here.

Finally, a true adventurer must always be lonely, if only in the sense that he has left his own country and his own folk far behind him. Every modern traveller knows that the farther the liner steams from the shores of England, the more wildly the clock in the smoking-room begins to differ from his wrist-watch, the more zestfully does that delicious feeling of adventure begin to steal upon his jaded senses. Mere distance—though it may sound

absurd — plays an essential part in all the best
adventures. The medieval troubadour returning to
his lady-love from Palestine had an important
advantage over rival lovers who had stayed at home.
And there is some indefinable greatness and aloof-
ness, a kind of gentle, godlike calm, about Englishmen who have lived in places beyond the ken of
ordinary men, which the rest of us can only humbly
bow before. These then are the essential elements:
physical danger; some pitting of oneself alone
against the fates; and distance from home. It may be
very arbitrary, but there it is. I am only trying to
give to the words, "the English adventurers," the
meaning that I know English readers will expect.
Remember, this is a book of adventurers, not of
heroes.

It is not possible, of course, to speak of the
English adventurers as we should speak of English
architecture, or the English common law. These
latter have, in the first place, continuity: their
history is one of growth or development from a
definite beginning. And in the second place they
have an insularity, a character of their own which
differentiates them sharply from the architecture
and the law of any other people. There is no
continuity in the story of the English adventurers—
unless we choose to begin at the reign of Queen
Elizabeth, and not much then. There is a gap, which
it would be mere verbal acrobatics to try and bridge,
between the Crusaders and soldiers of fortune of the
Middle Ages, and the Elizabethan merchant adventurers; and again between the merchant adventurers
and the great navigators and explorers of the

eighteenth and nineteenth centuries, who served the cause of science with as pure a heart as the airmen, motorists and other record breakers of to-day.

Nor—on the second point—is there anything in the English spirit of adventure which can be claimed as peculiar to our race. The English adventurer was driven forth by much the same motives as those which inspired the adventurers of other countries, even if these motives were somewhat differently mixed. At certain periods—to the Crusader or to the bewhiskered missionary—religion was the primary object, as it was (sometimes) to the Spaniards in the West Indies, or to the Portuguese in Abyssinia. The sword in one hand, and the bible or crucifix in the other! At other times we were frankly out for gain and nothing else, as the Dutch were in the Spice Islands. But the true source of inspiration, that divine curiosity about the world and its inhabitants which lies at the back of all travel and adventure worthy of the name, remained the same. And it was shared by the adventurers of every nation, whether they acknowledged it or not. We cannot distinguish the English adventurer by his motives. We cannot distinguish him by the character of his achievements, by the difficulties he encountered, or the hardihood with which he faced and overcame them. These things were common to all, and were part of our common European heritage. Indeed, to understand the essential solidarity of this diversified little continent a student might do worse than study the lives of the great adventurers.

Yet there is a difference after all. It is not what

the Englishman did—though he has done, perhaps, rather more than the rest, and over a longer period. It is not why he did it. It is how he thinks and talks about it afterwards. Being at once the most reserved and the most sentimental of Europeans, he is terrified lest posterity should ascribe to him some romantic, unpractical ideal. And since his real object, whatever it is, has become a romance to him, he is at pains to think of some other, and adopt it, and trot it out proudly whenever he is compelled to talk about himself. We get anything but the truth. The Elizabethans were never tired of assuring us that Eldorado was no dim city of their dreams, rising cool and lovely above the fever-stricken equatorial swamps, but merely a kind of strong-room or safe deposit out of which they proposed to extract money. Cook was going to open new trade routes; Livingstone's only idea was to convert the heathen; and to-day every time any-one climbs a bleak mountain, motors at a more dangerous and uncomfortable speed than any yet attained, or flies to some preposterous and useless height, we carefully assure ourselves of the practical business value of the exploit—without which, we infer, there would be no excuse for risking human life. If on the other hand, the object really is to make money (and is not gold the very stuff of romance?), then we say that, on the contrary, we were only trying to help the black men to lead happier lives, or to increase the sum of geographical knowledge.

And finally, the typical English adventurer always seems to travel with his chin on his shoulder.

He loves his home as much as any man, yet leaves it more readily than most. He takes some of his home with him wherever he goes, and never forgets it when he is away. If two Englishmen meet in the Sahara Desert, or among the Himalayan snows, it is long odds that in five minutes they will be talking of Piccadilly. Englishmen alone, perhaps, can fully understand what Mr. Chesterton meant when he made one of his characters walk out of his own front door and start off round the world in order to find his home. Fondness for travel is not only different from cosmopolitanism, it is almost its opposite.

One word as to the scope of this book. It is possible to begin with Boadicea, or with Hengist and Horsa. It is tempting to include the Norsemen, and point out that if an English ship (Cabot's) was the first to find the mainland of North America in Renaissance times, our Norse ancestors, as is now generally agreed, had been there some five centuries before and given it the name (oddly inappropriate to modern ears) of Wineland. But the ancestry of the English people has long been a question of acute controversy. As Mr. Guedalla once remarked, it is a wise nation that knows its own father. The simple theory of the nineteenth century, that the Saxon invader systematically removed all human life in his path, and that we made an entirely fresh start from then, is to-day gravely doubted. We apply a typical modern agnosticism to these dim periods in our rather shady past. All we know is that neither Celt nor Roman nor Saxon nor Dane nor Norman was a complete Englishman as we understand the word. The old historians tried to make us Germans; there is a modern school that makes us Roman-French. But I think we all know what is meant by "Englishman"—the very easily recognisable type that was produced by intermixing of these breeds. It was produced surprisingly quickly. It would hardly be going too far to say that by the date of the first Crusade, the national type was already known and distinguished. And since I am concerned here only with English adventurers, I propose to begin with the period of the Crusades. And by way of illustrating the futility of all attempts at precise definition, I shall have to begin with an English adventurer who violates all the rules I have just laid down, not only by setting forth under the orders of his king, but by being the king himself!

Of necessity this must be a very *personal* kind of book. It can only hold up a mirror to my own desultory and amateurish reading. It will ramble about the pages of history as I have rambled, and hope to ramble yet. The character of the subject precludes any other method. And since it is as impossible as it is undesirable to crowd our pages with mere lists of names, I apologise in advance for leaving out so many gallant and distinguished adventurers.

CHAPTER II

THE CRUSADERS

IN the Middle Ages it was an adventure even to make a journey to a neighbouring town. Conditions were so different that they are difficult for the modern Englishman to visualise. In the great walled towns there were guards at the gates, so that all who sought ingress or egress came under the eye of authority; in the outlying villages the houses huddled together for protection. In all the open countryside between, only a few lonely inns (often of sinister reputation) or an occasional baronial castle indicated the habitations of some scattered units of the comparatively sparse population of England. Wolves howled round the houses on winter nights, and sometimes, driven by hunger, would even enter the villages and pull down their victims in the streets.

The country had a strangely open appearance; for, in the first place, there were no hedgerows dividing the fields and adding charm and variety to the English scenery as we know it to-day; and, in the second place, all bushes and coppices were supposed to be removed from the sides of the roads, lest they should afford cover for highway robbers. A statute of Edward I laid it down that if there were ditches they must be so deep and so wide that they could not conveniently be used for this purpose. If the road crossed a park, the lord must enclose it by a high wall or a hedge too thick for a man to scramble through. Professional robbers were numerous enough on the high roads to be a public nuisance and could seldom be arrested, except when they ventured into the towns. Amateur thieves were probably equally numerous—landless men who might commit an occasional theft when food was short, or groups of evilly disposed persons who would waylay a neighbour, knock him down, and perhaps rob him, in pursuance of some village vendetta. Worst of all were the retainers of the great lords, who were the bullies of the countryside and could safely defy the law—unless they were unlucky enough to fall into the hands of the town magistrates, when even their powerful employer might find it difficult to save them. Some of the barons had professional robbers in their pay, and there would be brisk skirmishes on the high roads, with loss of life, between gangs of these ruffians and parties of peaceful travellers. Everybody went armed, and looked warily to right and left. In the *Paston Letters* alone there is material for several chapters on the perils of the road. Oh, yes; they travelled adventurously in those days!

Yet the strange thing is that they probably travelled more than at any intervening period between their time and the middle of the nineteenth century. There was a kind of life of the high road, which Chaucer has immortalised; there were types —mendicant friars, pilgrims, roadside hermits, pardoners, pedlars, messengers, merchants—who spent a considerable portion of their time on the roads, and, in some cases, looked to earn their living there. Among the causes of this incessant wayfaring, which made the medieval high road a moving panorama of the life of the time, first place must be given to the deep religious feeling of the age and the general belief in the spiritual virtue of making pilgrimages to the tombs of the saints. Pilgrimages were not only ordered by the priests as a form of penance (sometimes to be performed barefoot, or wearing only a shirt); they were regarded as highly desirable by all classes of the community. The sneers of Wyclif and Erasmus are of later date.

In England, there was the shrine of Thomas à Becket at Canterbury, famous for its miraculous cures. "For good people that are sick, Thomas is the best of physicians." There was the tomb of St. Cuthbert at Durham, of King Edward the Confessor at Westminster, of St. Edmund at St. Edmundsbury. There was the holy thorn tree at Glastonbury, the black marble cross at Waltham, and the wonder-working statue of the Blessed Virgin at Walsingham, which ranked only second to Canterbury itself. On the Canterbury road there was a regular service of hired horses, and rest-houses or *maisons-dieu* at intervals along the pilgrims' way. This road was also the usual highway to the Continent.

Foreign places of pilgrimage specially favoured by Englishmen were the tomb of St. James of Compostella in Spain, the sanctuaries of Rocamadour, Rome (which was regularly visited by Englishmen as far back as the reign of the Saxon king, Offa), and

Venice, where one might see the arm of St. George, one ear of St. Paul, the body of St. Mark, which had been brought all the way from Egypt, and a molar tooth from the jaw of Goliath.

At all these places English visitors were prominent. It must be remembered, of course, that there was in the Europe of the Middle Ages, a unity which does not exist to-day. Latin was a language common to all who could read and write, and every Englishman of the educated classes could also speak French. But, apart from that, the medieval Englishman was a great traveller, even as his descendants are to-day. Ralph Higden, the chronicler,[1] after commenting upon some of the less austere characteristics of the English, as, for instance, their delight in the pleasures of the table and in good clothing, continues in words which seem prophetic: "that people are curious enough that they may know and tell the wonders that they have seen; they cultivate other regions, and succeed still better in distant countries than in their own . . . wherefore it is that they are spread so wide through the earth, considering every other land that they inhabit as their own country." And Caxton remarks that "we Englishmen" were unfortunately born under the domination of the moon, "which is never steadfast but ever wandering."

The English, in fact, had already developed that appetite for "strange sights" which made Benvenuto Cellini, leaning over the battlements of the castle of San Angelo, watch with eager delight the

[1] Quoted in Jusserand's *English Wayfaring Life in the Middle Ages*.

sacking of Rome by the Imperialists, though he knew that his own house might at any moment go up in flames with the rest.

But the noblest of all pilgrimages, and the great inspiration of medieval travel in its most adventurous form was, of course, the Crusade. The English had considerably farther to go to reach the Holy Sepulchre than any of the other nations engaged in this high adventure. That seems to be the only reason why they played a less prominent part in it than, for instance, the chivalry of France. But the northern nations, no less than the southern, were stirred to their depths; and the general effect, here as elsewhere, was to give a great stimulus to that wandering spirit that Caxton had deplored. Listen to William of Malmesbury:—

"This ardent love not only inspired the continental provinces, but even all who had heard the name of Christ, whether in the most distant islands, or savage countries. The Welshman left his hunting; the Scot his fellowship with vermin; the Dane his drinking party; the Norwegian his raw fish. Lands were deserted of their husbandmen, houses of their inhabitants, even whole cities migrated. There was no regard to relationship, affection to their country was held in little esteem. God alone was placed before their eyes. Whatever was stored in granaries or hoarded in chambers to answer to the hopes of the avaricious husbandman, or the covetousness of the miser, all, all was deserted; they hungered and thirsted after Jerusalem alone. Joy attended such as proceeded; while grief oppressed those who remained. But why do I say remained? You might see the husband departing with his wife, indeed, with all his family; you would smile to see the whole household laden on a carriage, about to proceed on their journey. The road was too narrow for the passengers, the path too confined for the travellers, so thickly were they thronged with endless multitudes. The number surpassed all human imagination, though the itinerants were estimate at six million."

It must have been an amazing sight, that First Crusade. The East is familiar with the spectacle of holy wars; but in Europe nothing of the sort has happened, before or since. Peter the Hermit, the white-faced little humpback, who had been to Jerusalem and had seen how the Christian pilgrims suffered under the brutal rule of the Seljukian Turks, now rode ahead on a donkey, the mad light of battle in his eyes, waving on a motley herd of some hundreds of thousands of pilgrims, men, women, and children, all bound vaguely for Jerusalem by the overland route through Constantinople. Seven thousand are said to have survived to cross the Hellespont and invade Asia Minor. And of these only a heap of bones remained to tell of their bitter sufferings and of their hopeless fight against the trained Moslem armies, when Godfrey of Bouillon, Robert Duke of Normandy, and the other leaders of the main body of the crusading host arrived there with the regular forces in 1096.

Robert of Normandy, the Conqueror's eldest son, played a respectable part in the advance against Antioch, when he commanded one of the wings of the crusading host. He was present at the capture of Jerusalem, when the streets ran knee deep in blood, and the Crusaders exacted a terrible retribution for the persecution of Christian pilgrims during the past twenty years. How far Robert Curthose could be regarded as an Englishman (in spite of his English-sounding nickname) it is difficult to say. Probably he knew no more of the Anglo-Saxon language than would enable him to order his servants about; and the troops he took with him to Palestine would certainly not be English, but Norman-French from his own Duchy. On his return from the pilgrimage he became involved in war with his brother Henry, the successor of William Rufus, was defeated at Tenchebrai, and imprisoned for life at Cardiff. It is said that Henry had his brother's eyes put out—a wicked trick learnt from Byzantium. The Latin Kingdom of Jerusalem, founded by this first and most successful of the Crusades, lasted for eighty-eight years, when it fell before the conquering arms of Saladin and was never again in Christian hands until General Allenby walked on foot through Jaffa Gate at the head of his khaki-clad troops in 1917.

The First and Second Crusades had been directed against a number of more or less independent Moslem states, each jealous of the other, and some of them actually at war. But the suppression of the Fatimite Caliphate by Saladin, and the union of Aleppo and Egypt under one rule, surrounded the

Crusaders within a semi-circle of implacably hostile emirs, all acting under Saladin's orders, and forced them out of Jerusalem and back to the coast where they stood on the defensive, relying upon the reinforcements which continued to come to them across the seas from Europe. In 1188 when the news of the fall of the Holy City reached France and England, it was felt—and very rightly—that its recovery must be attempted at once if at all. Unless a new wave of enthusiasm could be set in motion, while the old crusading spirit was still alive, the situation in Palestine might become, as we say in modern parlance, stabilised: people might become accustomed to the thought of landing at a Christian port—Tyre or Jaffa—and then adventuring through an infidel land to the Holy Sepulchre and back: it might even add to the virtue of a pilgrimage. But Guy de Lusignan, the new King of Jerusalem, an active, unimaginative sort of person, was so far from accepting the *status quo* that he had collected all his available forces and laid siege to the port of Acre, which the Saracens had just taken; and there he was himself besieged in his lines by a powerful relieving army under Saladin in person. It was a critical moment in the history of the Crusades.

With the opportunity there arose the man. Richard Cœur de Lion of England may have used French as his natural language, but he was born in this country, and had an English foster mother, and the English nation took him to its heart from the start. He was the typical adventurer of the early Middle Ages—a very "parfit" if not a noticeably "gentil" knight—and by far the most dashing and efficient soldier who ever led the Crusaders in Palestine. And if the Normans and Englishmen who followed him just failed to recover the Holy City, it must be remembered that they won a series of resounding victories in the field against the best general the Saracens ever produced.

Richard was a man of magnificent physique, tall but not heavily built, evidently a born athlete, yet so muscular that there are innumerable legends concerning his feats of sheer strength. His hair and beard were "of a colour midway between red and yellow." Impulsive in temperament and recklessly brave, he was, like all the Plantaganets, subject to fits of gloom, and also to spasms of ungovernable rage. But he could be the best of companions, and the most simple and delightful of chiefs, so that it is clear that his men would follow him anywhere, and the only enemies he ever had were people of his own class. He never did things by halves. They called him "Richard Yea and Nay," not, surely, because (as some modern writers have suggested) he was a man of hesitation, but because his word was his bond and he knew his own mind. When he went into the Crusade, he went into it heart and soul. He took the Cross in France, in 1187. He heard of the fall of Jerusalem one night, and the very next morning interviewed the Archbishop. For the moment he could do nothing owing to lack of funds; but when his father died in 1189 and he became King of England, he thought of nothing else until the money had been raised, the ships chartered, and his fleet sent off by sea, while he himself started across France with a portion of his forces to embark at Marseilles.

The King of France, Philip Augustus, was to go with him, and at Tours they received from the Church the pilgrim's scrip and staff. Richard leaned upon his staff to test its strength, whereupon it snapped in two, and he had to be given another. At Marseilles the ships had not arrived, so, with characteristic impatience he pushed on round the coast and came to the south of Italy in September 1190. Here he had a typical personal adventure. Riding about the countryside, accompanied by only a single knight, he took a fancy to a handsome falcon which he saw in one of the houses, and, without stopping to think, dismounted from his horse, and went in and laid hold of the bird. A crowd of villagers assembled, and, when he would not give it up, assailed him with sticks and stones. One of them drew a knife, whereupon Richard, who thoroughly enjoyed a "scrap" of this kind, beat the man with the flat of his sword until the blade broke. He then took up handfuls of stones, and engaging the villagers at their own game, soon cleared the street of them and rode off safely with his companion.

In the Straits of Messina, Richard joined his fleet, which in a spirit of pure adventurousness had delayed its journey off Portugal, in order to help the Christians against the Moors. At Messina, there was trouble between the Crusaders and the inhabitants (there always was, everywhere in the East and in every Crusade), and there was a personal dispute between the King of England and the new King of

Sicily, Tancred. Richard's sister, Joan, was the widow of the former King of Sicily, who had left her a handsome legacy, including a golden table twelve feet long, with three golden tripods for sitting at the table, and a silken tent large enough for two hundred knights to sit and eat in. But Tancred showed no eagerness to produce these things; there was much ill-feeling; and Richard, while at dinner with the French King and some of his nobles, was interrupted by the news that the English were being murdered in the streets and the survivors of them driven from the town. He did his best to stop the rioting: he rode into the crowds, striking right and left with his staff, and ordering his men to disperse. But Philip of France did nothing. It pleased him to hear of English throats being cut, and he was all the time secretly negotiating with Tancred. So Richard suddenly stormed the town at the head of his English and Normans; whereupon Tancred hastened to make a treaty with him, leaving Philip out in the cold.

The crusading host was delayed all that winter at Messina, waiting for finer weather. The delay got on Richard's nerves. In friendly horseplay one day among French and English knights, all mounted but using bulrushes instead of spears, a certain William des Barres, with whom Richard had an old quarrel dating back to before the Crusade, charged upon the King of England, and broke his bulrush at the first thrust. Whereupon Richard behaved like a madman—or rather like a "black Angevin," as men said in those days; or like the Black Prince, his descendant, often did two centuries later. He charged the Frenchman furiously, but the shock only caused his own saddle to slip; whereupon he mounted another horse and renewed the attack, and might have committed murder if the Earl of Leicester had not intervened. "Get thee hence," he cried to des Barres, "and take heed that henceforth I will be an enemy to thee and thine for ever." It was not till many months later, on the battlefields of Palestine, that des Barres was restored to his favour.

After this unpleasant stay at Messina, which augured ill for the success of the Third Crusade, the French and English set sail for Palestine. But the latter were overtaken by one of those sudden Mediterranean storms which spring up from anywhere no one knows how, and their ships all scattered. Richard, who was "just as healthy and hearty, brave and strong, on sea as on land," had a powerful light hung from the stern of his ship. "Thus as a hen leads her chickens out to feed he led his mighty fleet."[1] But when he fetched up at Rhodes twenty-five ships were missing, and among them one which had on board his sister Joan, and Berengaria of Navarre, the lady to whom he was betrothed. That vessel, with several others, had been blown into the harbour of Limassol in Cyprus, and had met with a scurvy reception from Isaac Comnenus, the Greek governor, who had revolted against Byzantium, and set himself up as an independent ruler. He was hostile to the Christians in

---

[1] For this and other translations from the original authorities I am indebted to Miss Kate Norgate's *Richard the Lion Heart*, London, 1924.

Palestine, refused them supplies, and even made alliances with the infidels.

Richard hastened to Limassol, and found Isaac's army drawn up in hostile array to oppose his landing. He seized every ship in harbour, thereby more than making up for those he had lost in the storm, and then led a boat attack, himself springing waist deep into the water, and urging on his men, who, tired and seasick as they were, easily drove the Greeks before them through the town. Isaac mounted, and took to flight. Richard, dashing across the beach in pursuit, might have anticipated the cry of his namesake in Shakespeare's play—"A horse, a horse, my kingdom for a horse." Catching sight of a sorry country nag with a sack serving as saddle and stirrups made of rope, he jumped on its back and urged it desperately forward, shouting after Isaac, "Emperor, come and joust!" But Isaac had already seen more than enough of these hardy warriors from the North. He continued his flight, abandoning Limassol to its fate, and joining his own cavalry outside the town.

As the first horses were landed from the fleet, Richard hurriedly mounted fifty knights, and set off in pursuit. "They are too numerous," exclaimed a clerk who was with him, as the Greek squadrons came in sight. "Get you to your writing business, sir clerk," retorted Richard, "and leave matters of chivalry to us." Without hesitation he charged the enemy, shaking them severely, and, as more mounted Crusaders came up, the rout was soon complete, Richard capturing Isaac's standard with his own hand. The wretched "emperor" fled north to his capital of Nicosia. Richard returned to Limassol, brought Berengaria ashore, and married her in the chapel of a squat dark Gothic keep, which may be seen there to this day. They use it now as the local prison.

A few days of feasting, and he was off again, to the north, where he quickly completed the conquest of the island. Isaac was expelled, and Richard acquired his famous steed, Fauvel, and rode it afterwards in Palestine, where he, at any rate, was not mounted upon one of those heavy chargers, the use of which is said to have put the Crusaders at such a disadvantage as opposed to the swift Arab horses of Saladin's cavalry.

At Acre, when Richard arrived there, fresh from his island conquest, he found King Philip and the French already engaged in the siege, and the air full of intrigues against him. The events which followed need not be described in detail. Acre fell, mainly owing to the exertions of Richard, and when Saladin failed to carry out the terms of the treaty of surrender, the entire garrison was led out into the plain and mercilessly cut to pieces in sight of the Saracen army. Richard, as he rode into the conquered town, saw a banner already flying from one of the towers, and asked whose it was. He was told that it was the banner of Duke Leopold of Austria, who had captured that particular tower in one of the assaults. In a sudden fury he ordered it to be pulled down and trampled in the mud—a silly, bullying gesture, and one of evil consequence to himself.

King Philip had now only one idea—to return to France. He was of that type of crafty, self-seeking

Crusader, whose sole object was to acquire virtue by reaching Palestine, and then to hurry home and enrich himself at the expense of those who remained in the fighting line. So he made excuse after excuse, and at last he went. But many Frenchmen remained, and fought valiantly under Richard.

Richard, now in supreme command, prepared to march south to Jaffa, and from thence inland to the Holy City, the object of his dreams. He was a fine, romantic figure, as, mounted on his horse Fauvel, he rode up and down the Crusaders' lines, infecting them with his own enthusiasm for their sacred cause. Every man there knew that the King was the bravest among them, and the equal of the best of them in any feat of arms. They would not have been surprised if they could have foreseen the day when he was to re-capture Jaffa with only six mounted men at his back. As he stood up in his stirrups to address them, his red hair tumbled back beneath his square casquet, his chain armour carried as easily as if it were a silken vest, he must have seemed to them more god than man.

And the strange thing is that he appealed to the imagination of the East no less than to that of the West. The relations between Richard and his great opponent, Saladin, form one of the pleasantest episodes in the whole history of chivalry. To this day, parties of strolling Arab players may be seen in the streets of any town in the Near East, performing on a rough stage, in their own vernacular, a crude folk play about Saladin and Cœur de Lion, the main feature of which is the fabled visit paid by Saladin in disguise to Richard's tent, when the latter lay ill, in order that he might cure his gallant enemy's malady by the touch of a magic talisman.

Such was the lion-hearted leader of the Third Crusade, the first, and one of the greatest—if not the very greatest—of all English adventurers. He led his army southward along the sea coast in three thin lines, the infantry on the left, or inland side, the horsemen in the middle, and the baggage train next the sea. As Saladin's light cavalry pressed closer and closer against the column, the foot soldiers would open their ranks and the knights and squires would sally out, and drive the infidels back in headlong flight. In these encounters the sound of Richard's battle-cry was alone enough to make the enemy give way. At the battle of Arsuf, Saladin in desperation threw his whole army upon the Christian host, and was disastrously defeated by another great cavalry charge of heavily armed Englishmen, Normans, Frenchmen, Templars and Hospitallers, led by Richard himself mounted on Fauvel. We have a vivid account of the battle written from the Saracen side in which no attempt is made to minimise their staggering repulse. It was with difficulty that Saladin could ever again get his mounted warriors to face the Crusaders man to man.

Jaffa fell, and soon after Richard was nearly taken prisoner in a cavalry skirmish. Throughout the difficult advance on Jerusalem which followed, he (like Saladin) was constantly with the outposts and had a dozen hairbreadth escapes. On one occasion he came unexpectedly upon eight Saracens, slew three, and captured the other five. Another time, when leading a small raiding party, his camp was surprised just before dawn; but he himself was first out of bed and, armed only with a naked sword, led a vigorous counter attack which dispersed the assailants. In June, 1192, pursuing a party of Saracens, the King of England chased one of them to the top of a hill, and there slew him; and there, before he turned back to rejoin his companions, he got his first glimpse of Jerusalem far away in the valley below.

But there were serious dissensions in the Christian ranks, and so many other difficulties in the way that Jerusalem never was besieged. Whether Richard ever even saw it again is uncertain. De Joinville tells a story to the effect that after a retreat to the coast had been decided upon, one of Richard's knights cried to him to come to the top of a hill whence he might view the city. "Sire, sire, come here and I will show you Jerusalem." But Richard "cast his surcoat before his eyes all weeping, and said to our Lord: 'Fair Lord God, I pray Thee that Thou suffer me not to behold Thy Holy City, since I cannot deliver it from the hands of Thine enemies.'"

He had lost none of his personal prowess. The Arabs themselves relate that he would ride, lance in hand, along the whole front of the Moslem army, challenging any one of them to single combat, and that no man among them moved. In the height of battle they fled before him "as from the face of a furious lion." This was at his last great victory, at Jaffa, when he brought a few ships round from Ascalon to save the town, which Saladin had just taken by surprise, driving its garrison into the citadel. Richard, seeing the town crowded with Moslem soldiery, supposed that all was lost; but a certain friar in the garrison bravely jumped from the citadel walls, and falling in the shallow water near the beach was rescued by one of the English boats. He was taken to Richard's ship, which was "painted all red, with a red canopy on the deck, and a red flag," and Richard, no doubt, would be wearing his scarlet cap and mantle, embroidered with silver crescents and stars, which the chroniclers have described for us. When he heard that the garrison of the citadel was still holding out, he shouted for his sword and helm, and jumping half armed into the sea led his men ashore to one of the most surprising of all his victories.

But Philip was back in France and Leopold in Austria and messengers came to Richard from England to warn him that John was trying to steal his crown. His health was shattered, his money spent; he made an honourable treaty with Saladin and turned his face towards home. And here occurs perhaps the most inexplicable incident in the career of this delightfully "unexpected" King. He first set sail for Marseilles, which was like handing himself over to Philip bound; then changed his mind and contracted with a pirate vessel (no less!) to escort him up the Adriatic to Ragusa, whence he proposed to venture in disguise through a whole series of hostile states, including Leopold's, until he reached the northern seas, and England. It was a mad project. Why not go "long sea" by Gibraltar? It would be safer, and probably quicker in the end. No explanation of Richard's apparently lunatic behaviour has ever been advanced, except that he did it out of a pure spirit of devil-may-care.

Disguised as "Hugh the Merchant," he got as far as Vienna, after more than one mid-night gallop to escape from pursuing bands. But Leopold caught him then, and threw him into prison, and Philip hastened to the scene. Richard was brought before them, magnificently defiant. Nothing could damp his spirits. Moved about from one gloomy prison to another, he was "always cheery, and full of jest in talk," winning the hearts of his jailers. The King and the Duke, his two enemies, settled down to a prolonged period of negotiation, determined to extract from loyal England a medieval equivalent of the War Debt before they let him go.

England had fallen in love with him in his absence. The blandishments of John were of no avail. The Bishop of Bath, the Abbots of Boxley and Robertsbridge, were sent out officially to discover his whereabouts. A more famous emissary was the minstrel Blondel who (and there is no reason to doubt the story) played and sang beneath many a lonely tower before he heard the lusty voice of the Lion Heart answering his refrain through a barred upper window. Nothing of this kind ever happened to any other English king; but then no other English king was quite like Richard.

He got back to England in the end, became involved once more in the wars in France, was shot down by an arrow from the walls of a besieged town, and died, gasping out his forgiveness of the archer who had killed him. And that was the end of a great knight and a great gentleman, the first of the English adventurers.

CHAPTER III

THE FREE COMPANIONS

THE crusading spirit of the English did not suddenly evaporate with the death of their Crusader King, though it may fairly be described as gradually simmering down. Never again did a reigning English monarch lead an army to Palestine, but Richard of Cornwall was there in 1240, and there was the English Crusade of 1272, led by the heir to the throne, Prince Edward, who captured Nazareth, and slaughtered its inhabitants, but did little else. By the end of the century the great impulse had died down in the West.

Englishmen, however, continued to join the ranks of the Templars and the Knights of St. John, who maintained a precarious foothold on the sea coast of the Holy Land and afterwards on the islands of Cyprus and Rhodes. In the Street of the Knights at Rhodes may be seen to this day, carved in the stones above the doorways, the arms of noble English families, whose sons had given their lives to the service of the Cross. And many a knight afflicted by a vow made to Our Lady in some moment of peril, and many a robber baron seeking to ease his guilty conscience of some evil memory, and many a humbler sinner sent across the seas by his father confessor for the good of his soul, and many a noble exile, too, who had made England too hot for him, seeking some honourable employment until a change of government at home should permit of his return—all of these added something to the English share in the last dying efforts of the Crusades. Every one will remember Shakespeare's lines, describing the exile of Thomas Mowbray, Duke of Norfolk, banished from England by King Richard II after his quarrel with Bolingbroke:—

> Many a time hath banish'd Norfolk fought
> For Jesu Christ in glorious Christian field,
> Streaming the ensign of the Christian Cross,
> Against black Pagans, Turks, and Saracens:
> And, toil'd with works of war, retired himself
> To Italy; and there at Venice gave
> His body to that pleasant country's earth,
> And his pure soul unto his captain, Christ,
> Under whose colours he had fought so long.

But that was in the fourteenth century. Returning for a moment to the thirteenth, it should be recorded that it was not only knights and gentlemen who set forth on these adventures, and that it was not only to Palestine that they went. I imagine that even the boldest historian would hesitate to attempt any estimate, however vaguely worded, of the extent of the English emigration to foreign countries during this period. For me to attempt it would be a mere impertinence. But I carry in mind two statements from Villehardouin's narrative of that disreputable Fourth Crusade, which, instead of attacking the infidels, turned aside to pillage and destroy the

Eastern Empire instead. Villehardouin notes that, at the taking of Constantinople in 1204, the part of the wall which was most obstinately held against the crusading brigands, was defended by "Englishmen and Danes"—mercenaries, of course, in the service of the Byzantine emperor. These, at the first assault, cast the Crusaders out "in very ugly sort," keeping some as prisoners. And again, after the fall of the city, when the Crusaders who were still camped outside sent envoys to the young Alexius whom they had just placed upon the imperial throne, the chronicler records that "the Greeks had set Englishmen and Danes with their axes, at the gate and right up to the palace of Blachernae" and that the envoys, dismounting at the gate, walked through the streets between these lines of battle-axes. Such foreign service by Englishmen was probably much commoner than is generally supposed.

But with the fourteenth century, and the outbreak of the Hundred Years' War, the whole scene changes. For the first time since they became a nation the English are engaged in the wars of the Continent, and engaged in them "up to the neck." They make two important discoveries: first, that the day of the heavy armed cavalry is passed or passing; second, that they (the English) are, at the moment, the best soldiers in Europe. And the first of these discoveries must have surprised and rather shocked them; for in no nation in the world is respect for the officer and the cavalry man more deeply rooted. When our archers peppered the chivalry of France at Crécy and Poitiers so that they bristled with arrows like so many porcupines, or, to adopt Macaulay's metaphor, when the English lion turned at bay at Agincourt, and "trod the gay lilies down," no one who knows that sentimental animal can doubt that he did it with some secret feeling of regret.

But the second discovery—that they were the best soldiers in Europe—would not astonish them in the least, for lack of confidence on the battlefield has never been a national failing. It did, however, astonish the rest of Europe—almost as much as in 1815 and again in 1914—and the result was that English archers were greatly in demand in Brittany, in Spain, in Portugal. In every English village, men of humble origin were returning from the wars with loot enough to make them rich and envied by their neighbours. A class of professional soldiers sprang into existence. Men no longer drew the sword to fulfil a vow, or merely because their lord commanded them to. They entered the profession of arms for gain—and for the fun of it. It was, indeed, a great game. As we see it in Froissart's coloured pages, it seems to offer everything that a pugnacious imaginative people can want. And if, in other armies, the foot-soldiers—the "common sort" as Froissart calls them—were often ruthlessly butchered, or ridden down by their own cavalry, in Edward's armies it was not so. The archers were the backbone of that fine fighting instrument, and every one knew it. They, no less than the knights and squires advancing into the breach, were the King's "dear friends."

And then there came that disconcerting, futile, ephemeral peace of Bretigny, and (as after Amiens five hundred years later) all, or nearly all of these potential adventurers found themselves suddenly out of work. "Adventurers" in the most dangerous meaning of the word. They understood no other way of life, no other method of acquiring wealth and the means of leisure, except by seizing it forcibly from civilians—in short

> ". . . the good old rule, the simple plan
> That he should take who has the power,
> And he should keep who can."

It was thus that the Free Companions came into existence, to be a scourge to quiet, law-abiding men. And it is not for us who, after a war of only four brief years, found it so surprisingly easy to recruit our Foreign Legions and our Black and Tans, to blame our ancestors in the Hundred Years' War if they were a little over-stocked with adventurers of this type. Everybody knows Froissart's story of how, after Poitiers, there was "assembled together a great company of men of war of divers countries, such as lacked wages in other places"; for, "after the taking of the frenche Kynge they whiste not where to win anything in France."

So they went to Provence and pillaged the country to the very gates of Avignon. And "the Pope Innocent VI, and the Cardinals, being at Avignon [for this was during the Schism] had of that company great doubt," and kept a strict watch on the walls. But in the end they gave in, and entertained the leaders to dinner, and gave them formal absolution of all their sins—which were already many and soon to be more—and allowed themselves to be blackmailed to the tune of forty thousand crowns before they could get rid of their visitors. These "companions" included Englishmen, Gascons, Bretons, Navarrois—anyone who had been in arms against France.

"Also in the same season," says Froissart, "there rose another company of men of war of all countries gathered together; and they kept between the river of Loyr and the river of Seyne, wherefore none durst go nor ride between Paris and Orleans, every man fled to Paris: and the poor men of the country fled to Orleans." The leader of these companions was a Welshman named Ruffin, who, by robbery and pillage, had become "marvellous riche." "Some day they would ride near Paris, another day to Orleans, another time to Chartres," crossing an apparently empty countryside, silent and terrified. Twenty or thirty of them in a party would be enough to overawe such inhabitants as remained. Finally in Normandy was the greatest company of them all—in fact, it was called the Great Company—consisting of English and Navarrois, and "Sir Robert Canoll was chief of them." "This Sir Robert Canoll," says Froissart, "had long used like manner, he has well worth a hundred thousand crowns, and kept ever with him many soldiers at his wages; they pilled and robbed so well that many were glad to follow him."

Now "Canoll" is only the French way of writing Knollys, and Sir Robert Knollys, or Knolles, was undoubtedly an Englishman of good birth, though Jehan le Bel represents him as a German who started life as a tailor. Knollys was the brother (or possibly the nephew) of that almost equally famous leader of freebooters, Sir Hugh Calverly. Otherwise we know little of his early years, except that he served with credit in Normandy and under Henry of Lancaster. He appears for the first time as a leader of free companions in the year 1358. According to Jehan le Bel, Knollys, Reinault de Cervole and Ruffin, the Welshman, were the true originators and begetters of this new way of life. Knollys, after terrorising all Normandy, established himself in the Loire Valley, where he held forty castles and ravaged the countryside at will. Wherever he went he left behind him a trail of burning villages and ruined crops, so that the charred and blackened gable ends pointing to the sky came to be known as "Knollys' mitres." He had the impudence to burn the very suburbs of Orleans, and in this same year (1358) he took and sacked Auxerre and Chatillon sur Loing. At Ancenis the people threw themselves into the river at the mere rumour of his approach. When he carried his raids into Auvergne, the French made at last a serious effort to defeat and capture him.

> "Qui Robert Canolle prendera
> Cent mille moutons gagnera,"

wrote a contemporary versifier. But Knollys retreated before superior numbers, and, conscious no doubt of a certain lack of cordiality among his immediate neighbours, sent a loyal message overseas to the King of England, assuring the latter that all the castles in the possession of the Great Company were at his disposal. Edward III replied by formally pardoning Knollys for any robberies he might have committed on the King's subjects. Towards the end of 1358 Knollys was ambushed and made prisoner by the French; but his friends arrived in the nick of time and effected a rescue. A year later he retaliated by defeating and capturing the great du Guesclin and holding him to ransom.

After the peace of Bretigny, when it was no longer possible to pillage far and wide with any show of legality, Knollys entered the civil war in Brittany, taking the side of De Montfort against Charles of Blois. At once he appeared as what he really was—one of the ablest soldiers of his time. To him was largely due the final victory of De Montfort, who rewarded him with lands and money. Then, in 1367 came the great news that the Black Prince was at Bordeaux, preparing his famous expedition into Spain to restore Pedro the Cruel to his throne, and was appealing to all loyal Englishmen in France to rally to him. Knollys, who, as his worst enemies must admit, was always a patriot before he was an adventurer, hastened to join the standard. The late Sir Arthur Conan Doyle has pictured those stirring days at Bordeaux in the best book he ever wrote—*The White Company*. Knollys was a leading figure, and if the novelist's "White Company" was more or less mythical, it is a fact that Knollys was with Sir Thomas Felton at the first successful skirmish with the Spaniards, though he was fortunately absent on the date of Felton's defeat and death. At the final battle he distinguished himself by coming to the assistance of Sir John

Chandos on the left wing at the critical moment. He returned to France with the Black Prince, and—on the familiar principle of setting a thief to catch a thief—was given the task of suppressing the free companions in Aquitaine.

So far we get little idea of Knollys's personality, except that we are told that he was a man of few words. But now he was suddenly summoned to England and given the task of leading a raiding expedition into France with the idea of distracting the attention of the French King, who was understood to be preparing an invasion of Wales on an ambitious scale. This job just suited Knollys; starting from Calais, he swept across France like a pestilence, avoiding the towns, but setting fire to the farms and villages, so that the smoke was plainly visible from the walls of Paris itself. Seeing it, some of the French knights went to the King of France, Charles V, and urged him to send out an army to cut off this insolent raider; but he would not. This strange inactivity on the part of his enemies came at a fortunate moment for Knollys, for his expedition—though the French did not know it—was on the point of breaking up owing to internal dissensions. The young nobles objected to being ordered about by a former leader of irregulars; they began to talk about Knollys's rather shady past, and Sir John de Menstreworth, the chief malcontent, habitually referred to him as the "old brigand." Finally they and their followers broke away from him, and went raiding on their own account, only to be defeated and scattered by Bertrand du Guesclin. There were charges and counter charges in

England, ending in a complete vindication of Knollys's conduct.

We next hear of him at his own stronghold at Derval in Brittany which was besieged by the Duke of Anjou. There was some disagreement about the terms of capitulation, and the Duke, in a fit of rage, had all the English hostages executed. Whereupon Knollys brought out exactly the same number of French prisoners, slew them, and threw their bodies from the walls.

In July 1381 the old veteran was living peacefully in England, when the dangerous rising of the commons under Wat Tyler took place. Knollys was in London at the time (he had perhaps been driven from his Norfolk estates by the rebels) and witnessed the arrival of the mob and the amazing scenes that followed, when the Archbishop of Canterbury was murdered, and some of London's stateliest buildings went up in flames. While the maddened peasants raged through the streets, Knollys remained quietly in his home with a hundred armed men about him. Another old commander of free companies, Sir Perducas d'Albret, was doing the same thing a few streets away. And it was around these two that the citizens finally rallied, so that Knollys and d'Albret were able to bring a strong force to the support of the King at the fateful meeting at Smithfield. Every one knows the dramatic story of how Wat Tyler was struck down by the Mayor almost at the King's feet, and how young Richard II rode alone among the now leaderless mob and persuaded them to go quietly home. Froissart says that "Sir Robert Knollys was very angry that the rebels were not attacked at once and all slain." Other authorities assert, on the contrary, that it was he who persuaded the King to spare them. Froissart's version sounds the more likely.

This was Knollys's last feat of arms. He was now so rich that he was able to make loans to the young King, whom he survived by eight years, dying at a great age in 1407. But in 1398 he had found time to make a pious pilgrimage to Rome. Some years earlier than this, he and Calverly and Hawkwood had combined to propitiate the Church by founding the English hospital there.

Both the other members of this trio of repentant adventurers had carved out careers as romantic as Knollys's. Calverly and he had served together more than once—in fact they both first came into prominence at the celebrated "*Bataille de Mi-Voie*" or "Combat of the Thirty." In 1351 Robert de Beaumanoir sallied out from his stronghold of Chateau Josselin to take the town and castle of Ploermel, which was held for De Montfort by Sir Robert Bamborough and an English garrison. But before ordering the assault he sent a messenger to Bamborough with the very sporting proposal that, to save bloodshed, the quarrel might be decided by a duel between two chosen champions, to be fought out on the plain beneath the walls. Bamborough liked the suggestion, but proposed that a more satisfactory result would be obtained if each side put thirty knights into the field; and so it was arranged. There was a fine clash of arms, and at first the English knights, who had formed themselves in a solid phalanx, had all the best of it. De Beau-

manoir was severely wounded, and many other
Frenchmen were unhorsed. Then a single French
knight gallantly charged the phalanx and broke its
ranks, at which the English fell into confusion, and
all who survived, including Calverly and Knollys,
were made prisoners and held to ransom. Bamborough was among the slain.

Calverly afterwards went to Spain, and took
service with the usurper, Henry of Trastamare; but
when he heard that the Black Prince was at Bordeaux
preparing to support Henry's rival, King Pedro, he
at once crossed the border with his followers and
joined the English army. After the Spanish campaign we hear of him for a time in Armagnac at the
head of two thousand free companions. But his
activities gradually took on a more regular and
respectable appearance: he became Governor of
Brest and afterwards of the Channel Islands, dying
in the odour of sanctity in 1393. His effigy in complete armour is said to be one of the finest altar
memorials in his native county of Cheshire. He was
a bachelor and left no children, though there was a
romantic legend about his having been married to
"the Queen of Aragon."

But by far the most successful of the brilliant trio
of adventurers who founded the hospital in Rome
was Sir John Hawkwood, the lean, determined
Englishman with the hawk-like face, whose astonishing career in Italy reads like a romance, and who
now lies in the great Duomo at Florence where he
was buried at the public expense. That so little is
known of him here—that every English schoolboy
does not know the story of his adventures by heart

—is almost as surprising as the surprising facts of his life.

There is a kind of inverted snobbery which is always trying to prove that great men sprang from nothing. It was said of Knollys—untruly as we have seen—and it was said of Hawkwood. Hawkwood began his soldiering as a common archer, but his father, none the less, was of gentle birth. The son was with Edward III at Calais and with the Black Prince at Poitiers, and it was for his gallantry in the field that he was singled out for promotion and presently knighted. I do not think this often happened in the Hundred Years' War. Anyhow Hawkwood soon found himself in the usual difficulty of the ranker officer; he was reputed to be "the poorest knight in the army." He didn't like it, and when the Treaty of Bretigny was signed, and all pay and all looting abruptly ceased, it is hardly too much to say that an officer in Hawkwood's position had to choose between starving and turning freebooter. In his case the choice cannot have taken long.

With a chosen band of followers he marched southward and joined that large group of free companions, who, in 1362, completely defeated the regular French army under John of Bourbon which had been sent to chastise them. After the victory Hawkwood separated from the rest, and went on southward with his company to the River Po, plundering all the way, especially from the clergy, whom he seems to have disliked. He and his men were growing rich now, and more out-of-work soldiers from the north were constantly joining them, so that they soon numbered five thousand horse and fifteen hundred foot (mostly English archers).

They were called the White Company, probably in reference to their bright armour. We are told that "when they came to action their arms shone like looking-glass, and thus gave them a more terrifying appearance." On the other hand their discipline was, in some ways, remarkably slack; they camped when they felt inclined and seldom took the trouble to place sentries. When these English adventurers first came into Italy they scored heavily through their willingness to fight in any sort of weather, without going into winter quarters; but they soon fell in with the easy-going local customs in this respect, and before Hawkwood's death were as anxious to avoid discomfort or even serious fighting as any of the other foreign mercenaries that plagued Italy at this time.

Hawkwood himself is described as a tall, power-fully-built man, with a ruddy complexion, dark eyes, and a mop of chestnut hair. He first entered the service of Montferrat, but finding that the latter could not foot the wages bill, he enlisted himself and his men under the Republic of Pisa, then (as usual) at war with Florence. He had with him now one thousand lances, which means three thousand horsemen, for each "lance" consisted of a heavily armed knight on a charger, a less heavily armed squire, and a page on a palfrey. They did themselves well, these knightly freebooters. At first they won great glory for Pisa; but Florence offered heavy bribes, and Hawkwood waked up one morning to find his beautiful White Company reduced to eight hundred men; all the rest had gone over to the Florentine side, led by his former lieutenant, Hans Bongard, a German. He was outnumbered and defeated beneath the walls of Florence, and, to make matters worse, the two Republics made peace, and the mercenaries were disbanded.

But no mercenary who knew his business need starve in fourteenth-century Italy. The remnants of the White Company marched into Siena and Perugia, settling upon the country like a swarm of "fierce and greedy locusts," and ravaging it "in a dreadful manner." Hans Bongard was sent, in Perugian pay, to drive Hawkwood off; but the two leaders fraternised, and even dined together, ironically drinking the health of Perugia. At this time the majority of their men appear to have been Germans.

Hawkwood now entered the service of the Pope, and re-christened his company the Holy Company (1372). But the Pope turned out to be another bad paymaster, so Hawkwood seized and sacked Faenza, killing many people, and blackmailing the leading citizens. "Such dogs," exclaims Muratori, "did the Pope's ministers keep in their service." Hawkwood is further accused of being present at the massacre of Cesena, and of sending one thousand women of Rimini "to gratify the brutal desires of his followers." At the same time contemporary authorities are agreed that he was an unusually humane commander! He is often accused of avarice, but not of cruelty or oppression.

All this time he was secretly in the pay of Florence,

and, in the spring of 1380, in a return for a lump sum of 250,000 florins he formally went over to that Republic, in whose service he was to remain, and perform his greatest feats of arms. He had now three thousand lances and five thousand archers behind him. He was married to the natural daughter of Bernabo Visconti of Milan, with whom he had received a dowry of a million florins. He was rich, and so much feared that opposing generals would surrender towns at the mere rumour of his approach. Machiavelli refers to him as "an Englishman of great reputation in arms." There was a general feeling that, given evenly matched forces, he could always win—if he liked.

For one brief interval he left the service of Florence, but in 1387 he was back again, commanding the Florentine army in a new war against Siena. Galeazzo Visconti, the celebrated "Viper of Milan," and would-be dictator of Italy, who had poisoned his uncle (and Hawkwood's father-in-law) Bernabo and seized his dominions, supported the Sienese. It was decided to invade Milan from the south, while the French army, under the Count of Armagnac, co-operated with the north. Armagnac and Hawkwood were to endeavour to effect a juncture. But Armagnac was attacked separately, and defeated and taken prisoner; and Hawkwood, who had only 2200 lances and three or four thousand foot, was compelled to retreat before superior numbers. Venni, the Milanese commander, thought he had him cornered, and sent a messenger to the Florentine camp bearing a fox in a cage. Hawkwood let the animal escape and sent the empty cage back with a note to the effect that "the fox knew how to find his way out."

He did. He escaped by the River Oglio, his crossing being covered by a party of four hundred *mounted* English archers. (This is interesting, for the archers never fought mounted in France, and the longbow must have been an almost impossible weapon on horseback: indeed the Italian authorities assert that, even when on foot, Hawkwood's English archers had to drive the end of the great bow into the ground to steady it when they shot.) But Hawkwood's trials were not over; there was a sudden flood, his baggage was lost, and only a portion of his infantry was saved by holding on to the tails of the horses. However, Florence was astonished and delighted to see him back at all, and this retreat from Milan is generally regarded as his finest achievement.

Venni then invaded Florentine territory; but Hawkwood, though greatly inferior in numbers, out-manœuvred him, and pushed him back across the frontier. The war was concluded by the victory of San Miniato, when the Milanese were heavily defeated and lost two thousand men—an enormous figure for those days.

With the peace, all the captains of mercenaries and their men were disbanded, with one exception —Hawkwood. A wealthy and honoured veteran, enjoying a handsome pension, as well as his pay, he stayed on peacefully in Florence during the remaining years of his life (he died in March 1394). That excellent artist, Paolo Uccello, painted his portrait on the wall of the great church, above the marble monument, which was never, unfortunately, completed. The portrait has suffered by being removed from the plaster to canvas, but we can still see clearly that hawk-like profile, so finely cut, so expressive of the keen brain and the inexhaustible energy behind it. "Acuto," they called him in Italian, and he was well named. As I looked at this profile once in Florence, I found myself wondering where I had seen its like before. Lots of men like this I had seen somewhere. And suddenly a memory of the war came back to me, a memory of Gallipoli, a memory of long-limbed, lean-faced, eager men, men who love fighting (and looting, sometimes, too!), men of English stock, English adventurers. Yes, it is a curious thing, but this was an Australian face, if ever I saw one!

It only remains to add that there were also free companions of the sea. Throughout the fourteenth century and much of the fifteenth there were constant raids upon the coast towns on both sides of the English Channel. The Flemings, the Bretons, and the Spaniards all suffered severely at the hands of English raiders and were not slow to answer in kind. From among the English sea-captains who distinguished themselves in this irregular warfare I select one as typical—a certain Henry (or Harry) Page, whose home town was Poole in Dorset. The Spaniards, who were his chief victims, acquired a wholesome respect for this sportsman, whose name they rendered in their own language "Arripay." They supposed him to be a greater man in his own country than was actually the case. "Poole," says a Spanish chronicler of the first decade of the fifteenth century, "belongs to a knight named Arripay, who scours the seas as a corsair, with many ships, plundering all the Spanish and French vessels that he can meet with. . . . This Arripay burnt Gijon and Finisterra, and carried off the crucifix from Santa Uraria de Finisterra, which was famous for being the holiest in all these parts (as in truth it was, for I have seen it) and much more damage he did in Castile, taking many prisoners and exacting ransoms, and though other armed ships were there from England likewise, he it was who came oftenest."

The best retort the Spaniards could manage was a sudden raid upon Poole, when Harry Page's brother was killed, but the raiders repulsed. So strong was the feeling against this English filibuster that we are told that the raiders, before setting out, were formally absolved by the Church for anything they might do in Harry Page's native town in the way of murder, arson, robbery, and rape. And now, after all, I doubt whether Arripay has any right in this book. For all his enterprise and courage he was perilously like a pirate; and we are to have no pirates here.

CHAPTER IV

HAKLUYT'S HEROES

IN the fifteenth century the English adventurers, for the most part, stayed at home. Potential free companions, whether knights, squires or archers, were too busy cutting their own throats (in the Wars of the Roses) to attend to those of other people. In the second half of this century we were curiously cut off from the world. Though we fought all the time amongst ourselves, we fell badly behind in the art of war, because we had lost touch with the Continent, where the possibilities of artillery were just beginning to be appreciated with startling effect. It is, perhaps, something more than a coincidence that even our architecture, having arrived, like that of other countries, at the Decorated stage, should now have gone off on lines of its own and made an essentially insular and English contribution to the history of this art.

As for exploration, a man cannot travel and fight his neighbour at the same time. Bartholomew Diaz rounded the Cape of Good Hope—the culmination of a long period of Portuguese effort—only two years after the Battle of Bosworth Field, which finally settled the issue between York and Lancaster; and Christopher Columbus was in America almost before England had had time to take breath after her long internecine struggle. But though the heads of the old noble houses had been lopped off like so many poppies under the scythe, though the old nobility was dead and the appearance of English society permanently changed, there was a new generation growing up which needed only the opportunity and the release from internal feuds to prove itself at least as adventurous as any that had gone before.

We approach the great period in the history of English adventure—as of most English things. The great period, not only because the greatest things were done in it, but because they were better described. If the sixteenth century is the period of the greatest English travellers, it is also—and even more obviously—the period of the greatest English travel-writer. We can estimate roughly what we owe to Drake and Raleigh and John Smith of Virginia and Davis and Anthony Jenkinson and Hawkins and Frobisher and Hudson. But no one can estimate what Drake and the rest owed to their historian. I am not suggesting that Hakluyt's genius set these his heroes upon pedestals higher than they really deserved. I am only wondering how far they would ever have got their deserts without him. Without Hakluyt a whole gallery of glorious, intimate portraits might have been mere misty smudges. Without Hakluyt the full story of the Elizabethan adventurers could never have been told. And in any book about adventurers it seems only just that a chapter should be set apart for this greatest historian of adventure.

I think it was Mr. Belloc who once divided funny

stories into two classes—those which are funny simply because they are funny, and those which are funny because they are true. He might have gone further and applied his theory to stories of all sorts. Even then he would not have reached the central fact, which is that true stories have a particular quality, a manner and charm of their own, which distinguishes them from all others. "Truth is stranger than fiction," we say; and certainly its strangeness, its delightful unexpectedness, is one of the characteristics that mark it off most decisively from the manufactured climaxes of a modern novel.

But it would be better to say simply that truth is *different* from fiction—that it is not only stranger, but, in its own way, more beautiful, more moving, stronger, deeper, touching some chord in us that fiction can never reach. For we all can recognise a true story. We can recognise its *style*—what we call the "ring of truth." It is almost as though all true stories were written by the same author—which, indeed, when you come to think of it, they are. "This story, gentlemen, happens to be true," is an introduction which immediately arrests the attention of any audience. They turn eagerly towards you, as though you had mentioned the name of some favourite popular writer. It is obviously not a love of truth for truth's sake that moves them, but just a love of true stories—or of this particular style in story-telling, of which the vogue, in contrast with the changing fashions of fiction, began at the beginning and will last to the end. There is no need to labour the point: we shall have to return to it later. It is very apposite to our subject, because in Richard Hakluyt's *Principal Navigations, Voyages, Traffiques and Discoveries of the English Nation* we have probably the finest collection of true stories ever published in any language.

Hakluyt was, in Mr. Masefield's words, an "almost perfect editor," and the most honest of men. But when he assures Sir Francis Walsingham and the rest, in his Epistle Dedicatorie, that the reason why he undertook this work (which was really his life's work) was partly to bring more money into the Royal exchequer and partly to offer a cure for the unemployment problem, we may agree respectfully that these considerations no doubt sustained and strengthened his resolve, but we do not for a moment suppose that they were his real motives.

They were good cards to play at the time. The Queen always wanted money, and the unemployment problem, originally created by the suppression of the monasteries, had been rendered more acute by the inauguration of a period of European peace —or, at any rate, a reduction in the number of wars. The situation, indeed, was not unlike that with which we are trying to deal to-day. In a letter to Sir Walter Raleigh, written in 1587, advocating the colonisation of Florida, Hakluyt says :—

> Seeing therefore we are so farre from want of people, that retyring daily home out of the Lowe Countreys they go idle up and downe in swarms for lack of honest intertainment, I see no fitter place to employ some part of the better sort of them trained up thus long in service, than in the inward partes of the firme of Virginia against

such stubborne Savages as shal refuse obedience
to her Majestie. And doubtlesse many of our
men will bee glad and faine to accept this condi-
tion, when as by the reading of this present
treatise they shal understand the fertilitie and
riches of the regions confining so neare upon
yours [Sir Walter's colony of Virginia], the great
commodities and goodnesse whereof you have
bin contented to suffer to come to light.

He could hardly have put it lower. But we know
him better: we know that he is not stating his
motives, but is simply advancing topical arguments
in explanation of the appearance of his book, and
in defence of that passion for travel literature which
was already in him. For it is a curious fact that,
while we have so miserably little knowledge of
Hakluyt's life, we can trace the birth of this romantic
passion of his almost down to the very day and hour.
He has told us all about it himself. Hakluyt was
born of a good Welsh family (not Dutch, as his
name might suggest), either in or near London,
about the year 1553. On reaching a suitable age, he
was sent as a Queen's Scholar to Westminster,
"that fruitful nurserie," as he gratefully calls it;
and it was while he was there that the incident
occurred which was to have such a powerful
influence upon the rest of his life—and incidentally
to supply us, his descendants, with one of the
prettiest little pictures of daily life in Elizabethan
London that we possess.

"It was my happe," one day, he tells Walsingham, "to visit the chamber of Mr. Richard Hakluyt

my cosin, a Gentleman of the Middle Temple."
Now this elder Richard was a man of parts. He was
evidently a barrister of some distinction, for our own
Richard Hakluyt goes on to remark that he was
"well knowen unto you"—that is, to Mr. Secretary
Walsingham; but his practice was not so large as to
preclude a certain dalliance with subjects outside the
range of the law.

He happened on this occasion to be at home—
otherwise we should certainly never have heard of
him. Moreover, there chanced to lie upon his table,
or his "boord," certain "books of Cosmographie,"
together with "an universall Mappe," or map of the
world—it is impossible to guess which, for so many
were being produced at that time. Seeing his
young cousin "somewhat curious in the view
thereof," the elder Richard played up nobly. He
explained to the lad all the advances that had lately
been made in the study of geography—a subject
probably not included in the Westminster curriculum.
Warming to his task, he even took "his wand" and
pointed out with it all the "known Seas, Gulfs, Bayes,
Straights, Capes, Rivers, Empires, Kingdomes, Duke-
domes, and Territories of each part" with appropri-
ate remarks upon their commercial possibilities.

And after they had pored over the map together
for some time, "he brought me to the Bible," and,
turning to the 107th psalm, read out the well-known
passage about those who go down to the sea in
ships.[1] It was a gesture worthy of an Elizabethan,

[1] "They that go down to the sea in ships, that do business in
great waters; these see the works of the Lord, and His wonders
in the deep."

and it was a decisive moment in the career of Richard Hakluyt, the younger. We may hazard the guess that the elder Richard felt more than sufficiently rewarded by a glance at his young cousin's face. He little knew what he had done for himself. Thus is immortality conferred. It should be a lesson for all of us who have inquisitive young relatives at Westminster. Twenty-five years later Hakluyt wrote:—

which words of the Prophet together with my cousin's discourse (things of high and rare delight to my yong nature) tooke in me so deepe an impression, that I constantly resolved, if ever I were preferred to the University, where better time, and more convenient place might be ministred for these studies, I would by God's assistance prosecute that knowledge and kinde of literature, the doores whereof (after a sort) were so happily opened before me.

So the great idea was born. A few years later Hakluyt went up to Christchurch, where we know almost nothing of his career; but in 1577, after taking his M.A., he began at Oxford the first public lectures in geography that "shewed both the old imperfectly composed and the new lately reformed mappes, globes, spheares and other instruments of his art." What is known of the rest of his life can be very briefly stated. In 1583 he was appointed Chaplain to the English Ambassador in Paris, with instructions from Walsingham to keep a careful eye on the doings of France and Spain, and to make "diligent inquiries of such things as might yield any light unto our western discoverie in America." He lived in France for five years. He was a good French scholar—though not so fluent a speaker, he tells us, as his friend, Sir Walter Raleigh—and no doubt he used his time well. We know that he published several works, mostly concerned with travel, and had the honour of presenting one of them to Queen Elizabeth during a visit to London. But it was not until 1589, the year following his final return to England, that his *magnum opus*, *The Principal Navigations, etc.*, familiarly known to us as *Hakluyt's Voyages* saw the light. By that time he had been made a Prebendary of Bristol, in recognition of his work in France, and in 1590 he was instituted to the rectory of Witheringsett-cum-Brockford, in Suffolk, where he lived until 1602, largely engaged in his favourite "kinde of literature." In 1602 he probably moved to London, where he was presently made Archdeacon of Westminster; and in 1612 he took the living of Gedney, in Lincolnshire, where four years later he died, aged sixty-three.

He died just too soon. He left behind him sufficient MSS. to have formed another volume of his famous *Voyages*, but on his death this mass of material fell into the hands of Samuel Purchas, who published the greater part of it in his *Pilgrims* (1625), but completely ruined it by bad editing—clumsy cuts and abridgements, and unnecessary annotations. It is one of the little ironies of literary history that the most reverent, restrained and self-effacing of editors should himself have been so roughly treated.

What, then, was Hakluyt's method? It is not a

subject which he would dream of discussing himself. Our ignorance of his career would seem to him quite natural; an editor, he plainly indicates, should be a shadowy figure in the background, one whose personality has been allowed to merge itself in the work as a whole. We get but glimpses here and there. For instance, explaining the arrangement of his collection, in one of his dedications—how he has begun with narratives of Eastern travel and then moved over to the West—he mentions incidentally that such a mass of material is only to be got together after "huge toile" and "with small profit to insue," so that he now wonders at himself that he was able to do it. It involved, he says in another preface, "great charges and infinite cares," "many watchings, toiles and travels, and wearying out of my weake body." In the course of his description of "the voyage of M. Hore and divers other gentlemen, to Newfoundland, and Cape Briton, in the yere 1536," he remarks that "Richard Hakluyt of Oxford" rode two hundred miles across England to interview the only living survivor of this voyage, one Master Buts, and obtain the true account from him.

In some respects Master Buts's story is one of the least satisfactory in the book; it lacks colour, and even the air of truth, and our editor might have thought himself but poorly rewarded for his trouble were it not for the report of a remarkable oration by the captain of the ship, in which he appealed to his starving company not to fall into the horrible sin of cannibalism. It is plain that Hakluyt was prepared to test every story, by personal inquiry if necessary. We should have liked his own account of that two hundred miles' ride. Those were the days when, as Fynes Moryson tells us, England was famous for having the best inns in the world (it sounds impossible to modern ears!). We should have liked to have heard how Richard Hakluyt fared in them. We should have liked a description of the whole journey and of the people he met, somewhat in the manner of Froissart's well-known account of his ride across France to the court of the Count of Foix. We might even have sacrificed Master Buts's voyage for it.

But it would be idle to expect anything of the kind from Hakluyt; he was far too conscientious, too impersonal an editor. He *was* an editor, however, not a mere compiler. There is a justness in the arrangement and length of the stories which betrays the wise use of a blue pencil. There is a similarity in the information supplied by a large proportion (though not all) of the contributors, which suggests that Hakluyt may have sought to lessen his "huge toile" by the use of a fixed *questionnaire*. Moreover he has, in some vague way, not easy to define, impressed his own personality upon the whole collection and given it a unity apart from the subject matter. It is not the style—for that, as we have seen, is the style of all true stories. It is not the mere diction, for that is of the time. It is something more elusive; but it is there, and I should be surprised if any reader of the *Voyages* had failed to notice it.

One more fact about this extraordinary man, before we turn to the voyages themselves. It is that he never apparently attempted nor desired to visit

any of the countries which he dreamed and wrote
about and praised so earnestly all his life. He
represented Virginia as a land flowing with milk and
honey, but he himself was content to settle down
at Witheringsett-cum-Brockford, in Suffolk. He
had dedicated his life to "that knowledge and kinde
of literature,"—in fact to travel literature, not to
travel. Perhaps, tucked away somewhere at the back
of his mind, there may have been the fear of disillu-
sionment.

Confronted now with this magnificent array of
narratives, what adequate praise can any man give
to them, except to repeat stupidly that there is
nothing like them anywhere else in the world?
They range from Raleigh's admirably cool yet
sympathetic account of the last fight of Sir Richard
Grenville (he could admire, you feel, while he could
not quite understand) to the story of how that
equally great traveller, Anthony Jenkinson, nar-
rowly escaped with his life from the hands of
Cossack brigands on the borders of Persia—from
the classic description of the defeat of the Armada
to the daily journal of some half-educated sailorman.
Yet they are all alike in every essential quality. They
all have the same keen flavour of truth. They never
mention scenery, for instance, except incidentally.
All they seem to be trying to tell you is that there is
money to be made out of the "treyne oil" and furs
of the grey Murman coast, gold to be found in
rivers of El Dorado, oysters hanging in clusters on
the West Indian trees (Raleigh was one of the most
faithful believers in these oyster trees, as he was in
El Dorado, in the Amazons, and in the one-eyed

tribes). They paint the skies blue and set the palm trees swaying in the breeze, by pure accident, as it were. It is not the art that conceals art, but the art that is totally unaware of its own existence. "This," you say to yourself, "is where a stylist like Raleigh will fail: Raleigh unfortunately can write"—and indeed he can, much better than Hakluyt. But no such disaster occurs. Raleigh's dedications, of which there are many (the extent of Hakluyt's debt to him is not, perhaps, generally recognised), are written each in the manner of a set piece, in that wonderfully musical prose of which he was master. But as soon as he settles down to the narrative of a voyage, he becomes as simple and convincing as Jenkinson. A true story should be allowed to tell itself. The possession of an individual style in the narrator is a defect—an intrusion. It fogs and spoils the story, as popular actor-managers so often spoil Shakespeare. No such charge can be brought against Raleigh. It is difficult to quote from his narrations; but here is one of his rare descriptive passages, with an amusingly business-like twist to its tail:—

I never saw a more beautiful countrey, nor more lively prospects, hils so raised here and there over the valleys, the river winding into divers branches, the playnes adjoining without bush or stubble, all faire greene grasse, the ground of hard sand easie to march on, for horse or foote, the deere crossing in every path, the birdes towards the evening singing on every tree with a thousand severall tunes, cranes and herons of white, crimson, and carnation, pearching on the rivers side, the aire freshe with a gentle Easterly winde, and every stone that we stouped to take up promised either golde or silver by his complexion.

Which is not a bad summary of the general attitude of Elizabethan explorers towards the "new countries."

We are apt to forget the astonishing range of Hakluyt's collection. He promises us "voyages," by land and sea, but he gives us infinitely more. For example, in these volumes are included some of the most moving stories of captivity ever written. Miles Phillips's stolid, tight-lipped account of his appalling sufferings at the hands of the Inquisition in Mexico is something to be remembered—he seems to be setting his teeth as he writes. The night before the day appointed for judgment upon the English captives, "they came to the prison where we were, with certaine officers of that holy hellish house, bringing with them certaine fools coats which they had prepared for us, being called in their language S. Benitos, which coats were made of yellow cotton and red crosses upon them, both before and behind."

And in the morning, after breakfast, "we set foorth of the prison, every man alone in his yellow coat, and a rope about his necke, and a great greene Waxe candle in his hand unlighted," and so marched through the crowded Market Place of Mexico City to the scaffold, where they were made to sit down and hear judgment pronounced upon them, John

Gray, John Brown, James Collier and the rest of these Englishmen, "some to have two hundred stripes on horseback, and some one hundred, and condemned for slaves to the gallies, some for six years, some for eight, and some for ten." "Which being done, and it now drawing toward night, George Rively, Peter Momfrie, and Cornelius the Irishman were called and had their judgment to be burnt to ashes, and so were presently led away to the place of execution in the market place but a little from the scaffold, where they were quickly burnt and consumed." Miles Phillips himself was sent to serve as a slave in a monastery, from which he eventually escaped.

Nowhere do we realise more clearly than in the pages of Hakluyt the bitter hatred inspired by these "devildoms of Spain." Cruelty, indeed, was the prevailing vice of the brilliant sixteenth century—a thing quite shocking and inexplicable to this present age. An Englishman, Lionel Plumtree, travelling in the Middle East, could record with evident satisfaction that certain "Cassaks" who had made a piratical attack upon his ship, being captured by the local authorities, "were put to most cruell torments, according to their deserts."

Thus does Hakluyt, setting out with no other intention than to interest us in foreign parts, reflect most vividly the Europe of his day, in all its weakness and its strength. The lighter side is pleasantly prominent; we may discover little touches of unconscious humour on almost every page. In the course of John Davis's first voyage for the discovery of the North-west Passage, he landed a party with instructions to "allure" the natives to them. Their idea of doing this was to "make a great noise," causing "our Musicians to play, ourselves dancing." Apparently the natives were highly pleased by this lively demonstration, which nowadays would be considered extremely bad for the white man's prestige. We get some curious sidelights upon their idea of a suitable diet for the tropics. Every man was allowed a sinful quantity of beer, and one of the principal reasons for the abandonment of Frobisher's last voyage was the fact that his casks were running dry. "All the way homeward they drank nothing but water," says the chronicler plaintively.

But it is impossible to indicate the greatness of Hakluyt by a series of disconnected quotations. It is not a question of this passage or that, but of the cumulative effect of the whole. Indeed you cannot find anywhere in the *Voyages* a passage that can fairly be called "typical." His book is as varied in pattern as life itself. One moment you are drifting in a canoe down a South American river with painted savages shooting at you from the banks; the next you are one of a huddled group of sheepskin-clad merchants on a snow-swept plateau in the Middle East, calling upon your comrades for one last charge upon the Turkish brigands who gallop round and round, like vultures circling round a corpse. One moment you are the half-naked slave of some Algerian bey; the next you ride dignified, in furs and velvet, in the train of an English Ambassador to the Muscovite Tsar.

Always you jot down notes about the trade

openings for English goods, the commercial possibilities of the country. This Master Richard Hakluyt of Oxford, who has asked for a record of your experiences, is particularly insistent upon that (yet his eye lights up strangely as you recount some adventure by the way). You are traders, of course, nothing else—plain English merchants from Norwich and Bideford and Rye. Never will you acknowledge that craving that is within you to find out everything, to know and experience everything, to hug all the New World to you—roses and thorns alike—in one eager, fierce embrace. You do not pause for self-analysis. You are of the sixteenth century, when the world was suddenly young again, and the morning stars sang together—perhaps for the last time.

All this Hakluyt has faithfully transcribed for us. He succeeded because he had the right idea. He could not fail. He knew that the truth was sufficient for his purpose—that no one who really wanted to know what Englishmen had done in the past would begin by reading *The Charge of the Light Brigade* or would turn to Tennyson's *Revenge* for the best account of the death of Grenville. He set himself patiently to dig for and disinter the romantic truth itself. And if we could follow his method to-day, if we could hunt down every adventurous voyager by land or sea and make him tell his story simply, in his own words, then—allowing for all the disadvantages of our greater geographical knowledge, our decayed prose style, and the effect upon the narrators of our meretricious "education"—there can be no reasonable doubt that we should again produce a book which future generations would hail as one of the greatest of our time. It would not be too big a book. In attempting to estimate Hakluyt's achievement, we must remember not only what he included but what he left out. He must have had a fine sense of discrimination. And it may be added that his contemporaries showed an equally fine discrimination (which their descendants have not always succeeded in imitating) when they accorded Hakluyt the honour of a burial in Westminster Abbey.

.   .   .   .   .

Hakluyt's heroes put to sea in clumsy, unhandy little ships, upon pirate-infested seas, with crews composed mainly of land-lubbers, and no proper instruments to assist them in fixing their position or keeping their course. The *Golden Hind*, in which Drake circumnavigated the world, was no doubt a handier vessel than any galleon of the Spanish Armada. Yet, considering her to-day, it seems a wonderful feat of seamanship to have navigated her even to America. These Elizabethan ships were not even beautiful: they had not the *line* from fo'c'sle to counter, which is the essential line of beauty in a ship. They were high charged above the water fore and aft, with a low waist breaking the line between (we do not get full two-deckers till the eighteenth century). But the English built their fo'c'sles much lower than their poops, and this was undoubtedly an advantage from the point of view of seamanship. It did, however, give the effect of a stumpy fat little duck, constantly toppling forward on to his beak.

It gives the sailor's word "beakhead" a new significance, and helps us to picture the misery of these gallant crews trying to shelter under canvas coverings in the waist from the seas which the little ship seemed deliberately to sluice over her back, as she pushed her beak into the waves.

These awkward little vessels in which such great deeds were done appear to have been brightly painted in a great range of colours. To me it has always been one of the strangest mysteries of history that it is so hard to recover the colours of the past. That sound should be lost—the music of the Greeks, for instance—is nothing remarkable, for there was no way of writing it down. But why do they never tell us about colour—or hardly ever? How can we see them without? Only recently there has been a newspaper controversy about the colour of the eyes of Mary Queen of Scots. Contemporary evidence is contradictory. Well, I suppose if they were so hopelessly vague about the bright eyes of the loveliest woman of their time, we can hardly expect them to have been more explicit about the paint on their ships' sides. It would seem, however, that the hulls were painted green and white in stripes, black and white, red, or timber colour; the gun decks were green or red (as in Nelson's time) and the interior of the cabins green. The red Cross of St. George flew at the main.

A three-masted ship would have two square sails on the foremast and mainmast and one on the mizzen. They had neither jibs nor staysails to help them to work to the windward: the only head-sail they possessed was the little square sprit-sail, set beneath the bowsprit, which always has such an oddly unexpected, irrelevant appearance in the pictures of these ships. The tallest mainmast would not be more than seventy to eighty feet high, and a ship of three hundred tons was reckoned an exceptionally big one. The food consisted of biscuits, salted meat, and cheese, with a daily allowance to each man of one gallon of beer a day. That makes about sixteen glasses—but then no one ever thought of drinking water in those brave days! Unfortunately the beer was often acid, the cheese mouldy, and the meat bad. The importance of fresh food as a preventive against scurvy and dysentery was not understood until well over a century later.

I do not suppose that Drake himself, nor any English admiral two weeks out from home, ever had a meal served at his table in the grand cabin which would not cause an immediate mutiny if offered on the lower deck of one of His Majesty's ships to-day. On the other hand, the Elizabethan crews, who suffered these hardships without a murmur, were quite startlingly lacking in ordinary *esprit de corps*. There was always a large proportion of them ready for any mutiny or intrigue. Not the greatest of their leaders, not Drake himself, could command unswerving loyalty. No age has talked more about loyalty and practised it less. Their horror of the crime of treason, which has coloured so many pages in the English Prayer Book, was simply due to the fact that treason was one of their besetting sins.

The captain, of course, was responsible for the discipline (he was often a landsman, who knew nothing of navigation: the master looked after that) and a good sixteenth-century captain knew just how to deal with these sixteenth-century Englishmen. He would put the mutineer in chains, strip him, starve him, bully him for weeks, tie him up to the mainmast (as John Hawkins did) and stand in front of him with an arquebus ready to shoot him dead for his crimes. And then, with a gesture learned from Shakespeare and Marlowe, he would throw down his weapon, and, bursting into a flood of tears, would fling his arms round the prisoner's neck and proclaim him a free man and his beloved brother. But he would keep an eye on that man's conduct ever afterwards.

Such were the men, and such the means they employed during the greatest period in the history of English adventure. It remains to indicate briefly the extent of their achievements.

CHAPTER V

DRAKE AND THE NEW WORLD

A STRONGLY built man of middle height, with wide shoulders and immense depth of chest, curly hair and short beard, a broad good-humoured face, arched eyebrows, a humorous mouth, and a mad merry light in his eyes that boded well for his friends and ill for his enemies. English writers describe his hair as dark, but to the Spaniards he seemed a fair man. There is also an unusual quality in his face, which I might have found it difficult to describe, if Mr. E. F. Benson[1] had not done it for me. In all the portraits, Mr. Benson notes, there is "a look of alertness and surprise, as if he had just learnt something of high and rather gleeful interest, and was eager without delay to act on it and prepare, perhaps, a surprise for somebody else." "Gleeful surprise" exactly describes it; you can see that the man is startled but without being in the least bit disconcerted. It is easily the most wide-awake face in the Elizabethan picture gallery. The thick unruly curls descend low upon the forehead; the bearded chin is thrust a little forward. He would have made a fine Crusader, you reflect, or a great rider to hounds. The very type and embodiment of an English man of action—such was Francis Drake.

[1] *Sir Francis Drake*, by E. F. Benson. London (Lane), 1927.

We need not waste much time over the ancient argument as to whether Drake, Hawkins, and the rest were pirates. Smugglers, of course, they were. The primary object of their voyages to the West was not simply to arrest Spanish ships and steal Spanish gold (though that might happen), but to open up a new market for English trade—to secure some reasonable share in this New World, which the Spaniards were trying to monopolise, so that any-one who sold an old hat or a yard of cloth to the Indians was treated by the local governors as a smuggler and an outlaw. It is true that Drake and his fellows did much harm to the Spaniards at times when England and Spain were officially at peace; but, in fact, all the seafaring nations of the world were continuously at war with Spain in this matter.

It has been well said that a man is only a pirate if his contemporaries agree to call him one. In Elizabeth's reign every English sailor was a pirate to the Spaniards, but it is certain that no French-man or Dutchman—no man of any other nation — would have dreamt of applying such a term to Drake. Drake was a man of his time, neither more nor less moral in his private life than most men (though with a special gift for swearing, which many of his shipmates have paid tribute to) and neither more nor less respectful of legal forms. He never did anything that any English-man need feel ashamed of, nor that any of his contemporaries, except the Spaniards, thought of blaming him for.

Magellan's ships were the first to circumnavigate the globe: but Magellan died on the way, and it may be claimed for Drake that he was the first admiral to leave his home port at a given date, and return to it, in the same ship, having ploughed a furrow round the world. The *Golden Hind* sailed from Plymouth on 13th December 1577; she arrived there again, with Drake still on board, at the end of September, or early October 1580. It was, without a doubt, the most momentous voyage ever carried out by an Englishman.

With regard to Drake's antecedents, it is necessary to remember that (though he was never a religiously minded man) he was the son of a zealous Protestant who had been driven from his native town in Devon in the reign of Queen Mary, and had been obliged to make a new start in life somewhere in Kent. Young Drake was educated at the expense of his kinsman, Sir John Hawkins. He had all the religious and political prejudices that might be expected from such a start in life. He made his first important voyage in command of the *Judith*, which formed part of Hawkins's fleet at the disastrous affair of San Juan de Ulua in 1567, when the Spaniards made a sudden and treacherous attack upon Hawkins's little force, and, by that means, brought off one of the few successes they ever scored against our ancestors. Drake got the *Judith* out of harbour less damaged by gunfire than any other ship in the English fleet; and having done that he set sail for England, leaving the rest to look after themselves. But loyalty to the admiral in command was never a strong point with Elizabethan sailors, and Hawkins, though he did make one reproachful reference to the *Judith's* desertion ("she forsook us in our great

misery") never seems to have borne any grudge
against his young kinsman.

In 1572 Drake had again visited the Spanish
Main, in command of only two small vessels, with
which he performed incredible exploits, taking and
sacking the town of Nombre de Dios, loading his
men with plunder, smashing the images in the
churches, and finally setting out with a land expedition to cross the Isthmus of Panama—the first of a
long succession of predatory Englishmen (including
many of the most picturesque and ruffianly of the
buccaneers) to perform that feat. He had climbed a
tall tree on the isthmus and had seen the wide blue
Pacific at his feet, and had prayed earnestly to
Almighty God to give him life and strength to sail
an English ship upon that sea. (Among his company was young John Oxenham, who did it before
him, and died in the effort). And he had gone on to
the coast near Panama and ambushed and taken the
Spanish treasure trains, the pack-horses struggling
under loads of bar gold, of richly chased ornaments,
church furniture, jewelled sword hilts and all the
fabled wealth of the Aztecs. And had staggered
back again through the forests and the swamps till
they reached the Atlantic and re-embarked, and
finally arrived at Plymouth on 9th August 1573,
with such a cargo as fired men's imagination, and
loosened even the royal purse-strings for any future
expedition Drake cared to undertake.

It was on 13th December 1577 that Drake set
sail with five small ships on the voyage that was to
take him round the world. That great feat of seamanship formed no part of the original project,

which was to pass through the Straits of Magellan, destroy the Spanish fleet in the Pacific, and plant a strong English colony in Peru. With this ambitious scheme in view, the *Pelican* (afterwards re-christened the *Golden Hind*) and her consorts were unusually well equipped and victualled. Drake himself travelled like a king. He dined off silver, while fiddlers played soft music behind his chair; and often might be heard through the ship the imposing roll of Drake's drum—that same painted drum which he carried all round the world with him, and which exists to this day. In person he was magnificent, for he loved to strut in fine clothing, and had, moreover, a shrewd perception of its effect upon the native potentates and small Spanish governors.

In July 1578 they were within a few days' sail of the Straits of Magellan. It was here that the much-discussed execution of Thomas Doughty took place. Doughty had been Drake's friend, and he loved him dearly; but when his friend was discovered to be plotting a mutiny, Drake's love changed to a deadly hate and he could not rest till the traitor was dead. Yet five minutes before his head was struck off, these two Elizabethans knelt together, side by side, at Doughty's own request, and received the Holy Communion from the chaplain. Another five minutes and the executioner was holding up Doughty's bloody head before the assembled crew, while Drake looked gravely on.

In September they reached the Pacific, thus fulfilling Drake's ambition. But they ran into terrible weather, and were dispersed by storms, and first one ship and then another disappeared or returned to England, until Drake found himself alone. He sailed north along the coasts of Chile and Peru, plundering Spaniards, and "beseeching God, the Saviour of all the world, to have us in His keeping, to whom only I give all honour, praise and glory." But as he went the Spaniards rose behind him and armed ships poured out from their harbours like angry bees from hives that have been insolently disturbed; so that it was obviously impossible to return to England by the way that he had come. Drake therefore continued northward, in the hope of finding that fabled North-west Passage which has cost so many English lives.

Failing in this, there was only one route open to him—to cross the Pacific to the East Indies and the Cape of Good Hope, and get back to England, so to speak, from the other side of the world. This is what he did. The Spice Islands were sighted in September, just a year after passing through the Straits of Magellan. On 15th June the *Golden Hind* doubled the Cape of Good Hope, having then on board only fifty-seven men (the expedition had started out more than six hundred strong) and three casks of water. In July they were off Sierra Leone, and in September (just another year again) they sighted the Azores, having apparently been blown somewhat out of their course. And on 26th September (or, as some think, early in the following month) the gallant little vessel entered Plymouth harbour.

Drake's great voyage must be taken as typical of the rest. It was not the end of his personal adventures; he had yet to "singe the King of Spain's beard" in the Bay of Cadiz; serve against the

Armada as Lord Howard's second in command; lead the fleet in an indifferently successful expedition against Portugal; and finally die at sea while engaged in the one complete failure of his career—the ambitious expedition against the Spanish West Indies in 1594, in which he and Hawkins shared the command and quarrelled all the time.

Hawkins also died on this unhappy voyage. It is astonishing that even the least imaginative Government official should have supposed that two leaders, so utterly different in temperament and method as Drake and Hawkins, could run together in double harness. The figure of Hawkins has only recently been divested of the Victorian fustian in which nineteenth-century writers had clothed him. In place of the crude, unkempt old sea-dog, with his mahogany complexion, his hoarse, bellowing voice and his insatiable thirst, whom Charles Kingsley sketched for us in *Westward Ho!*, there now emerges a quiet, precise, methodically minded official and merchant-adventurer. Hawkins had only one taste in common with Drake—a love of finery. Indeed he once nearly lost his life while walking in the Strand, through being mistaken by a would-be assassin for the courtier, Sir Christopher Hatton—the greatest dandy of his time. In all his American adventures his methods were precisely the opposite of Drake's. He did not treat the Spaniards as his enemies; indeed it was his whole object to open up a friendly trade with them. And it was for that reason that he began shipping negro slaves from Africa (thus becoming the founder of the slave trade), because he knew that the Spanish colonies were short of labour, so that the Spanish governors could seldom resist his blandishments in spite of King Philip's orders against any kind of commerce with the English heretics. If Hawkins were alive to-day, I think he would rather resent seeing his name in a book about "adventurers."

It must be remembered that among these Elizabethan adventurers in the West, there were some who thought first of booty, some of peaceful trade, some of geographical discovery, and some of colonisation. The greatest of the colonisers was John Smith, the founder of Virginia. This resolute, red-headed man, with his bristling beard, had all the faults of his age. He was once nearly hanged for mutiny, and was probably about as unsatisfactory a lieutenant as a ship's captain could wish to have. But he was, by nature and instincts, more a soldier than a sailor, and when he found himself on the shore, in supreme command of that forlorn little band of colonists in Chesapeake Bay, he showed such qualities of leadership as give him a place of his own in any history of our Empire.

But Smith's most resounding adventure, one which may be taken as the type of a whole class of adventure stories, and has inspired more romance than, perhaps, anything that ever happened to an individual Englishman, occurred some time before the Virginian colony found its feet. Smith and a few companions were on a boating expedition, looking for food, when they were attacked by Indians, and Smith was taken prisoner. For many weary weeks he was led about from village to village and exhibited to the inhabitants.

At last it was decided to kill him, and his head was already on the block, while the executioners swung their clubs to dash his brains out, when the Indian chief's beautiful daughter, Pocahontas, rushed forward, and, flinging her arms round the white man's neck, laid her head upon his, and refused to move until the chief agreed to grant his life to her. She afterwards prevailed with her father to let Smith go free. It is a pretty story, which, in the late nineteenth century it was rather the fashion to sneer at, though there is no real reason for doubting it. Smith was an upstanding young fellow of twenty-eight, and Pocahontas was a girl of fourteen. This was the first white man she had ever seen, and she ever afterwards remained our friend, being converted to Christianity, and using her influence to prevent attacks on the little colony at Jamestown.

Another coloniser was Sir Walter Raleigh—the most attractive, baffling, and yet impressive figure of them all. He is unique in the history of adventurers and men of action in that he really seems to have preferred the life and the art of the courtier to that of the soldier, the sailor, the explorer, the poet, or the historian, at each of which, with amazing versatility, he was equally proficient. The profession of courtier is thought little of to-day—the word is almost a term of reproach—but at the Court of Queen Elizabeth it was cultivated as a fine art by men who were artists to their finger-tips. Let us not too hurriedly blame Raleigh for his preference. As we saw in the last chapter, his story of his search for El Dorado is among the classics of travel literature.

El Dorado, that mythical city of gold and silver rising abruptly from the South American jungle; Terra Australis, that vast southern continent which existed only in the imagination of our ancestors, and was to go on existing there until well into the eighteenth century; the North-western Passage between the Atlantic and the Pacific, the existence of which seemed as obvious to the Elizabethans (if only they could find it) as the Straits of Magellan at the other end of the newly discovered continent—these were the three lures that drew adventurers from every part of the civilised world. And the most insistent of them was the idea of the North-west Passage. At the very dawn of the century, King Henry VII, that shrewd man of business, had been attracted by the idea, and the main object of the voyages of the Cabots had been to find a route by which English merchandise might be carried direct to the East Indies, and even to far Cathay, without the trouble of rounding the Cape of Good Hope. When John Cabot landed on the coast of Labrador, he at first thought, like Columbus, that he had arrived in Asia. In the reign of Henry VIII, Robert Thorne, the merchant and map-maker, used all his influence and much of his wealth to encourage a series of more or less successful voyages with this object in view, but the King's active interest in maritime affairs was limited to the building up of his navy, and nothing much was done in his time, nor in that of his son, while Queen Mary was obviously handicapped by her matrimonial alliance with King Philip of Spain, who regarded all English sailors in American waters as pirates.

With the accession of Queen Elizabeth the search for this impossible North-west Passage was taken up with renewed zest. Humphrey Gilbert, Richard Hakluyt, Richard Willes, and John Davis wrote vigorously on the subject, adducing innumerable "proofs" of the existence of the passage. The great Mercator himself wrote to his son that there could be "no doubt but that there is a straight and short way open into the west, even unto Cathay." The first important voyage was undertaken by that able navigator, Martin Frobisher, backed financially by his friend Michael Lock, by Anthony Jenkinson of the Muscovy Company (whom we have met before), by Lord Burghley and Mr. Secretary Walsingham, and by the Earl of Leicester, the Queen's favourite. Frobisher, a rough and ready adventurer, who came nearer to deserving the name of pirate than any of his contemporaries, collected a small fleet of ludicrously inadequate little ships, and dropped down the Thames past Greenwich, on his way to China. Queen Elizabeth, then in residence at Greenwich, saw from her window these cockleshells upon the water and asked where they were going. To Cathay! She seems to have been pleased with the reckless courage of this foolhardy enterprise, for she sent a message to the captain inviting him to call at the palace next day, and bid farewell. (June 1576.)

Yet Frobisher, with his eggshells, reached the coast of Greenland, and there one ship sank, and another deserted and went home. In a single vessel he continued his voyage to Baffin Land and the bay now called Frobisher Bay; and though he found no North-west Passage, he returned home with some lumps of quartz which the more optimistic of his backers believed to contain gold. He never made another attempt upon the North-west Passage, but Humphrey Gilbert did, and failed like all the rest, and died on the homeward voyage.

The greatest of the sailors who wasted their lives on this hopeless quest was John Davis—a shadowy figure, of whose exploits we have a bare record. He got well into Baffin's Bay, and if anyone could have forced a passage through those ice-bound waters he would have done it. But of his personality we know next to nothing. There is little material, and above all, too little "human interest" in the known facts of his career to attract the attention of historians. He sailed again with Cavendish (the same who distinguished himself by capturing the Manila treasure-ship) and made, altogether, three voyages, but never found Cathay. In his last voyage he brought home only sixteen of the seventy-six men who had started out with him. He has left his mark upon the map in the Davis Straits. He was killed by pirates in the East Indies in 1607.

In 1610 Henry Hudson set forth on his famous voyage. There is good reason to believe that others had entered Hudson Bay before him; but he was the first to make it known to the world, and, by his tragic death there, he earned the right to some memorial. There are few more melancholy pictures in the whole history of English exploration than that dismal scene under the grey northern skies, when Hudson and his few loyal companions, hurriedly wrapped in the warmest cloaks they could find, were pushed off from the ship's sides in a small boat, to the accompaniment of jeering farewells from the mutineers, to drift away to a lonely, lingering death among the ice-floes. The mutineers, on their return to England, were brought to trial for this abominable crime, and unaccountably acquitted.

Baffin made his first voyage in 1516. Again we must admit that he was not the first to enter the bay which bears his name, for John Davis had been there; but Baffin explored and mapped it. His greatest distinction lies in the fact that he was the first to announce to a shocked and disappointed world that the North-west Passage was a myth. That was really the end of the quest, though Foxe and James, setting out independently in the year 1631, reached northern waters, and there, after fraternising together, came to the conclusion that, if the existence of the Passage was doubtful (James frankly disbelieved in it), the whales alone were sufficiently numerous and valuable to attract English sailors.

Turning now from the New World to the Old, let us glance at the activities of the merchant adventurers of the Muscovy Company, who traded along the Murmansk coast, and made inland voyages to Moscow and as far as Persia and the Middle East. They had no gift for publicity, these Muscovy merchants. Their names, compared with those of Drake and Raleigh, Smith and Hudson and Grenville, are simply unknown. Borough and Chancellor (who was drowned at sea), Plumtree and Anthony Jenkinson are known only to readers of Hakluyt, who form, after all, but a small proportion of the modern public. The dramatic element is lacking in their enterprises. To open up a new trade in treyne oil or furs against an exchange of English cloth, even to dine with the Czar himself at Moscow or join the caravan to Aleppo and the south, seemed less exciting to their contemporaries than the discovery of new straits and islands, or the capture at one stroke of a Spanish ship laden with a cargo of gold. The result is that we know nothing of them, except what Hakluyt tells, and even Hakluyt seems to feel a little chilled and sobered when he turns towards the East.

Taking that sturdy traveller, Anthony Jenkinson, as typical of the rest, it must be confessed that he does nothing in his narratives to dispel this impression. His style is that of a grocer making an inventory; nothing that he sees in his wandering holds any interest for him apart from its commercial possibilities. In 1557 Jenkinson commanded the ship *Primrose* in a voyage to Russia. In 1559 he returned from a visit to Bokhara, and wrote a long account of it, which Hakluyt has preserved. He was evidently a man of forceful personality, for he had a habit of getting his own way and was respectfully treated wherever he went. He was in such favour with the Czar that Elizabeth appointed him her ambassador, and he obtained many privileges for English merchants in Persia and the East.

But even Jenkinson's essentially business mind cannot conceal the romantic character of his undertakings. Scattered through his narrative are little glimpses of adventure in different parts of the world which are worth any amount of search among Hakluyt's crowded pages. Some day, no doubt, the adventures of these "eastern" Elizabethans will be "written up" as they deserve.

The death of Raleigh in the opening years of the seventeenth century (29th October 1618) seems to mark most fittingly the close of this greatest period in the history of English exploration and adventure. He stood smiling on the scaffold. Perceiving a bald-headed man among the crowd, he threw him his cap: "You need this, my friend, more than I do." He made a short speech. He had been ill, and was suffering from ague, and was anxious to explain that his fits of trembling were not due to fear. He answered once more the charges that had been brought against him, and then asked all present to pray for him:—

I have many many sins for which to beseech God's pardon. Of a long time my course was a course of vanity. I have been a seafaring man, a soldier, and a courtier, and in the temptations of the least of these there is enough to overthrow a good mind and a good man.

It might almost stand as an epitaph upon the Elizabethans.

The executioner, deeply moved, came forward and asked for his forgiveness. Raleigh patted the man on the shoulder, and told him he forgave him with all his heart. Many years before he had written the famous lines beginning "Oh eloquent just and mighty death"; and now he picked up the axe, and running his finger along it said smilingly: "This is a sharp and fair medicine to cure all my diseases." To the audience he said once more, "Give me heartily your prayers, for I have a long journey to go." Refusing to be blindfolded, he lay down and placed his head upon the block. Many of those present were in tears. The executioner seemed to hesitate. "What dost thou fear?" said Raleigh, speaking for the last time, "Strike, man, strike!" And so at last the axe fell and severed the head of one of the ablest and bravest Englishmen that ever lived. And with that stroke ended the brilliant, theatrical, conquering century which Raleigh in his own person seemed to epitomise.

We see the men of that century every day achieving the apparently impossible, launching forth without hesitation upon voyages from which, as they very well knew, less than half of them might reasonably be expected to return; with crews composed largely of ignorant landsmen who looked forward to encountering sea-serpents, men with heads beneath their shoulders, giant savages seven or eight feet high, and a dozen other horrors enough to deter demi-gods; we see them quarrelling among themselves, their gentlemen volunteers (who were often more trouble than they were worth) intriguing against the captain, their clothing unsuitable and their food hardly fit to eat; and we see them succeeding in spite of all. In many different parts of the world, under many purple, tropic skies, racked by sickness and fatigue, they lay on their backs in their cockleshell boats, staring up at the stars and dreaming. Great dreamers, great poets, great adventurers.

CHAPTER VI

THE BUCCANEERS

IF centuries could speak, the seventeenth would probably complain that the sixteenth was an uncommonly difficult century to follow. King James and King Charles might very well protest that in all the troubles of their reigns, economic and political, they were but reaping the whirlwind sown for them by those self-satisfied Tudor despots, whom historians have agreed to acclaim as successful statesmen (and if handing on your problems to the next in line marked "passed to you, please" constitutes statesmanship, they certainly deserved the name). In art and letters who could hope to maintain that first fine careless rapture of the Renaissance? The characteristic product of the seventeenth century in England was not the great artist, but the great connoisseur. In the magnificent collections of King Charles I and Lord Arundel, the hard brilliance of sixteenth-century work is succeeded by the gracious portraits of Vandyke and Lely. The organ notes of Elizabethan literature give place to the charming verses of the Caroline poets.

It was not only in the field of geographical discovery that the sixteenth century had found a new world at its feet. It was, however, most obviously and literally so in that field. There was

America—a stupendous new fact. There was the route to the East. It was becoming apparent that the North-west Passage was either non-existent or impracticable; and when the Dutch rounded Cape Horn in 1616 it really seemed that there was nothing more to do.

But the seventeenth century did not sit still. Since it seemed that there were no new countries to discover (for the continent of Australia, as we know it, was not yet even a dream), the explorers of this century concentrated on discovering new things about countries the existence of which was already known. The map of the world had undergone, within the memory of living man, such a re-modelling as we can hardly imagine to-day. It was speckled with new countries of which almost nothing was known except their names, but as to which European governments and traders, and (be it noted) the whole European reading public, were consumed with an eager curiosity. There were still plenty of openings for the English adventurer, and, except for that disastrous break in the middle of the century when the King and the Parliament were at death-grips, he did not fail to take advantage of them. Ship-building design improved under the intelligent patronage of the Stuart kings; navigation was studied; and, before the end of the century it became possible for the first time to take a reasonably accurate observation at sea.

But new types of adventurers had come into existence. The game of filibustering still had its devotees, and, as we shall see, was presently to develop in the West into a wide-spread and dangerous profession. The merchant adventurers of the Levant and the East Indies were still risking their lives daily and sending home those cold, business-like reports, such as Hakluyt used to collect, setting forth the various commodities which might be profitably disposed of in different parts of the world. But there arose now a type of traveller whose object was not (even ostensibly) trade or booty, but to see as much as possible of the world. He travelled for travel's sake. He expected, if he returned home alive, to become a person of some note—and so, no doubt, to improve his income. Sometimes he even set out on his travels with the deliberate intention of writing a book about them and making money out of it. This is quite a new phenomenon. We see here the prototype of the modern travel writer who goes about in odd places with a camera and a fountain pen, and finances each new expedition on the proceeds of the book which he (or she) wrote about the last.

The best example of this new kind of adventurous traveller is Thomas Coryat. In the first two decades of the seventeenth century there was quite a rush of Englishmen to the Near and Middle East and to India, and most of them found their way, by one means or another, to the court of the Moghul Emperor. There was Robert Fitch (1583-1591), who was sent out to make a report to Lord Burghley and was imprisoned at Goa by the Portuguese; John Mildenhall (1599-1616), who wrote a long letter home which he may or may not have intended for publication, and who now lies buried under the oldest English gravestone in India; William

Hawkins (1608-1613) and John Jourdain (1608-1617) and William Finch (1608-1611), all of whom kept excellent journals; Nicholas Whittington (1612-1616), who undoubtedly intended his narrative for publication, if only to justify his own attitude towards Mildenhall and other Englishmen; Edward Terry (1616-1619), who wrote an elaborate treatise for the Prince of Wales; and lastly, the Thomas Coryat aforesaid, who was already well known as a travel writer before he made his Indian voyage and sent home from Agra his long and entertaining epistle, which he would undoubtedly have published if he had ever got back. Of these eight, four died in the East and one on the way home—and when we consider the conditions of eastern travel in those days, the only wonder is that as many as three survived.

Coryat was an eccentric, and the son of an eccentric. His father, who was parson of Odcombe in Somerset, had from boyhood a fatal facility for the writing of bad Latin verse. While still a scholar at Winchester at the age of fourteen, he addressed to Queen Elizabeth, who was visiting that town, a set of verses in which he urged her to take a husband at once. Elizabeth gave him five pounds for the effort. He also translated all the Psalms into Latin. He bequeathed his impudence and his taste for Latin to his son, but happily not his lack of wit. Young Thomas went to Oxford in 1596, but characteristically left without obtaining his degree, though he was a good scholar and possessed a remarkable memory. He attached himself to the court of Elizabeth, and, according to Fuller, was treated as a kind of buffoon, "the courtiers' anvil to try their wits upon." But he often gave harder knocks than he received. It is said of him that he carried folly in his very face: "the shape of his head had no promising form, being like a sugar loaf inverted, with the little end before, as composed of fancy and memory without any common sense"— a charge that might be brought against a good many adventurers. Ben Jonson has a story of how Coryat was packed up in a trunk, and suddenly produced in the middle of a court masque, to the great amusement of the assembled company.

On his father's death in 1608 Coryat suddenly disclosed his real quality. Having now a little money, he left England and undertook a walking-tour—surely the first on record!—through France and Italy, and home *via* Switzerland, Germany and Holland. The result was a book entitled *Coryat's Crudities hastily gobbled up in Five Months' Travels*. Unfortunately this entertaining work failed to find a publisher, until Coryat went round to all his courtier friends and induced them to write laudatory verses for his preface. Most of them sent in absurd mock heroics, treating the matter as a joke, and this amazing farrago of nonsense was edited for Coryat by no less a person than Ben Jonson, and may be read in the few remaining copies of the *Crudities* to this day.

This book had a very large sale—which probably surprised the jesters, but was well deserved, for it was easily the best book of its kind. Coryat, with replenished purse, immediately left England on his memorable journey to Greece, Asia Minor, Egypt,

Palestine, by caravan to Mesopotamia, and thence to India and the Great Moghul's court. He was four years upon the road, and during that time learnt to speak Persian, Turkish, and Hindustani; he knew Sir Thomas Rowe, our ambassador to the Moghul, and was better treated and appreciated by this distinguished diplomat than by the courtiers at home. The letters in which he describes his adventures and sufferings on this journey were written from Agra; they take a high place in our travel literature. Alas, Coryat's iron constitution, which had survived such hardships as few other travellers could endure, was not proof against the hospitality and good cheer of the English merchants at Agra and Surat. He died at the latter place in 1617, of a flux brought on by too much good living. It was the gallant buffoon's last jest.

It is impossible not to like Coryat, and even—as a travel writer—to believe in him. He says he saw two unicorns at the Moghul's court, "the strangest beasts of the world." Why not? Why assume, as one distinguished critic does, that these beasts were "of course rhinoceroses"? Coryat's testimony is supported by that of dozens of other writers of different nationalities. If the evidence of men's senses can prove anything it has proved the existence of the unicorn. To say that the animal is "anatomically impossible," as the scientists do, seems to me wretchedly weak. It is like the attitude of mind of the little boy at the Zoo, who, upon being shown the giraffe, exclaimed "I don't believe it." Poor Coryat's great ambition was to have his portrait taken as he sat on the back of an elephant—a thing

he had often done. Death intervened. But it is
pleasant to know that his publisher, who made so
much money out of him, later produced an imaginative picture showing a gaily dressed cavalier, in
plumes, jack-boots and spurs, perched perilously on
the back of a much-dramatised elephant.

Need I add that the names of these wanderers in
"the unfrequented Inde" do not exhaust the list
of English adventurers in the first half of the
seventeenth century? There was, for instance, that
unfortunate traveller, William Lithgow, who was
captured by the Spanish Inquisition and so cruelly
tortured that when he got back to England King
James I sent for him, and he was carried to Theo-
bald's on a feather bed that His Majesty might
inspect his "martyred anatomy." When Lithgow
got well enough he went to Court and assaulted the
Spanish Ambassador with his fists, for which he got
nine months in the Marshalsea—but probably
thought it worth it. He published two accounts of
his travels, one of which sold well, and he seems to
have undertaken his later journeys with the deliberate intention of making money out of them in
this way. But his literary work is not nearly as good
as Coryat's, who was the first travel-writer in the
modern sense of the word. And there was that
amazing man, Adams, who might have written the
most wonderful travel book of all. Serving before
the mast on a Dutch ship, he is cast ashore on the
coast of Japan. Making his way to the court of the
nearest local potentate he shows them how to build
ships (how many common seamen could do that
to-day?), and so impresses his personality upon

every one he meets that he is presently one of the most powerful men in the country, upon whose word hangs the fate of many a European trading concern, many a Dutch skipper-owner of a merchant ship, many a Jesuit mission. And at last, near the end of his life, when he has got permission to go home and is about to realise that long frustrated dream of seeing once again England's green fields and of hearing his native language spoken in the streets, he stays to perform one last task and dies, and so misses his dream after all.

And perhaps we may note here that there were English soldiers of fortune fighting in Germany on both sides in the Thirty Years' War (1618-1648). And Scots too—it is a serious consideration that from now on, the two Crowns being united, we must begin to include Scottish adventurers in our list.

But it must not be supposed that while there was all this high endeavour in the East, nothing was being attempted by Englishmen in the West. If there had been anybody to make a tally of the adventurers' ships as they put out from the home ports, I fancy he would have found a surprisingly large proportion of them bound for the Americas. Only in the West the effort took a different, a more individual, undisciplined, lawless turn. And this was not our fault, but entirely the fault of the Spaniards, with their dog-in-the-manger policy which denied to all the rest of the world the right of trading with this vast continent, in the discovery of which Columbus had only beaten Cabot by a short head.

The result was inevitable. Every man's hand in the West was against Spain. Sometimes the English Government would be formally at peace with Spain, sometimes at war; but among the islands of the West Indies and upon the Spanish Main there was a perfectly clear understanding—even clearer on their side than on ours—that between England and Spain, as between France and Spain, Holland and Spain, Denmark and Spain, there could never be peace in that hemisphere. It was as though someone should lay claim to one half of the air, lacking the skill and courage to patrol it in support of this preposterous claim, possessing only the malevolence to imprison and torture any helpless airman who happened to make a forced landing.

It was from this state of affairs, deliberately created by the Spaniards themselves, that the power of the buccaneers arose. And, since this is a book about adventurers, it is desirable to sound an early note of warning against the too easy acceptance of the popular view of those very remarkable adventurers. We all know that view. The buccaneers are first discovered upon the island of Haiti (or Hispaniola, as it was then called) hunting the wild cattle and boars and salting down the meat in places called *boucans*, from which comes their name. They never wash, but steep their garments in the blood of the slaughtered animals. They go armed to the teeth, and will murder a stranger on sight. They drink prodigiously, indulge in every vice, and are, in short, a blot upon the fair face of the Golden West.

At first they are mostly Frenchmen, numbering

three or four hundred all told. But when the Spaniards turn upon them and drive them out of Hispaniola and Tortuga, every foreign adventurer in the West Indies, every landless man, every shipwrecked mariner or escaped slave hastens to join them. Under Mansvelt, who seems to have been the first to organise them as a fighting force, John Davis of Jamaica, L'Olonois the Frenchman, and Henry Morgan—a really great leader—they became a power to be reckoned with, both on land and sea. They sank Spanish ships and burnt Spanish towns, roasting the citizens over slow fires to make them disclose their hidden money-bags, ravishing their wives before their faces, and slaughtering their children. L'Olonois, in an access of bestial rage, ripped open the breast of a prisoner, tore out his heart and gnawed it savagely. No wonder Andrew Lang describes the buccaneers as "the most hideously ruthless miscreants that ever disgraced the earth and the sea."

But the plain truth is that most of these lurid details depend upon one single authority—that of Esquemeling, the Dutchman. Esquemeling, who landed in Hispaniola in about 1669, was an unwilling recruit among the buccaneers, who at that time could not aspire to the comfortable and even regal style of living which they afterwards attained in the days of their power. He hated the life, and he hated his companions, and when he got back to Holland it did not need a hint from his publisher to induce him to "write up" the horrors of buccaneering in the approved modern manner. It is simply impossible to believe that Charles II could have knighted

Henry Morgan and made him Lieutenant-Governor of Jamaica, or that similar recognition should have been accorded by their Government to several French buccaneers, if one half of the charges brought against these leaders by Esquemeling were true. Still, if we believe only half of them, the buccaneers were hardly adventurers of the idealistic, unselfish type, devoted to the cause of Christianity or of geographical knowledge. As one of their chroniclers frankly states, they were inspired by no higher motive than "the sacred hunger of gold," and "'twas gold was the bait that tempted a Pack of merry Boys of us, being all Soldiers of Fortune," to undertake the particular buccaneering exploit which he proceeds to relate. Yet even in their case, and though they may not have known it themselves, I suggest that gold was only the lure in the sense that money is the lure at a game of bridge. The game was the thing.

Incomparably the greatest of them was Henry Morgan. This distinguished Welshman, worthy descendant of Ruffin, the Free Companion, was not, as Esquemeling alleges, a run-away slave from the plantations, but a youth of decent family who had gone to the West Indies as a soldier. He must have been a man of tremendous personality, for he seems to have been able to persuade the governors of Jamaica to back him in almost anything he did, and his authority over the mixed collection of adventurers of all nations who followed his flag was undisputed until he cheated them at Chargres by bolting with the loot. At one time he commanded a buccaneering fleet of over fifty sail.

For his personal appearance I accept the portrait in the Dutch edition of Esquemeling's book, though it cannot, of course, have been taken from life. It shows us a burly, red-faced man, wearing the long love-locks of the period, with upturned moustache and a neat little imperial, dressed in a handsome, slashed doublet—for the buccaneers, like Drake and Hawkins, had an eye for colour and loved to strut their decks like peacocks. There is a heavy jowl and a brutal mouth, surmounted, unexpectedly, by two large and beautiful eyes— which may sometimes have assumed the terrifying appearance of cat's eyes to his trembling prisoners.

Morgan's most resounding exploit (the only one we need describe here) was the capture and sack of the wealthy city of Panama, in whose harbour the great treasure galleons cast anchor before setting out with their precious freights across the southern seas. To accomplish this, he had to transport his little army from the Atlantic to the Pacific, across the Isthmus of Panama—a place notorious even to-day for its abominable climate, its swamps and impassable rivers, its mosquitoes and alligators and poisonous snakes. To have crossed it at all, in the presence of hostile forces, was no inconsiderable feat; but when Morgan's exhausted followers at last saw before them through the palm trees the white roofs of Panama, they sprang forward to the attack with such *élan*, such reckless disregard of death, that nothing could stand against them, and soon the streets of the city were running in blood, and the buccaneer leaders were seated in the council chamber sharing out the rich booty of gold bars and doubloons, altar vestments, crucifixes and silver candlesticks. There was the wine too; but Morgan, with characteristic cunning, had solemnly warned his men that every barrel had been poisoned by the fleeing Spaniards, and by this means had always a sufficient force sober enough to carry arms.

The buccaneers returned slowly across the isthmus with their booty, leaving Panama in ruins. It was then that Morgan left his followers in the lurch, and slipped quietly away to Jamaica with most of the loot. He was received like a returning hero. In the following year (1672) he went to England and stood his trial for piracy, when he was triumphantly acquitted amid the plaudits of the populace. Returning to Jamaica, he was appointed Lieutenant-Governor and held this honourable post for the remainder of his life, though he seems to have been an unconventional kind of official, who spent most of his time, according to a confidential report from his immediate chief, Lord Vaughan, "frequenting the taverns of Port Royal, drinking and gambling in unseemly fashion." He died in his bed, and they gave him a first-class funeral at the public expense.

About the time of Morgan's conversion to respectability a treaty was concluded between England and Spain whereby the latter agreed that English colonists and traders in the West Indies should be allowed to continue their peaceful avocations in those places where they were already settled without being treated as outlaws and pirates if they fell into Spanish hands. This treaty obviously meant the end of buccaneering as a possible career for a gentleman. In the meantime, however, the

Spanish authorities failed to implement it. If they caught an English ship at sea they would imprison the crew without inquiry. Or they would sell them into slavery, as they did with poor Captain Buckenham, who was last heard of staggering about the streets of Mexico City with a heavy log chained to his leg, crying bread for his master, a baker.

The result of all this was that though the buccaneer's profession was really doomed and the day of the common or garden pirate[1] was near at hand, Morgan's immediate successors were of a type rather better than those who followed him to Panama. The number of English in the West Indies was increasing. We had ten ships there in 1670 for every one before the Civil War. Nothing could stop that movement. At the same time it had become plain for all men to see that in seamanship and gunnery the English were immeasurably superior to the Spaniards, so that the danger of sailing in those seas was considerably decreased.

Man to man, too, there was an equally obvious, if temporary, advantage. (I say "temporary," because the fighting weight of nations goes up and down; only a hundred years before this the magnificent Spanish infantry overawed all Europe and no one knows what might have happened if the Armada had been able to put its soldiers ashore.) In the meantime one English buccaneer was worth a dozen South American Spaniards. To go "on the account," as it was called, was fatally easy for an

---

[1] The right buccaneer fought as Morgan did under his national flag; the pirate under a disreputable blood-red rag or the traditional skull and crossbones.

English seaman, while at the same time the rapid increase in immigration made it less easy to obtain an honest job ashore. Dampier, the typical buccaneer of this transition period, was driven to join the "privateers"—another contemporary euphemism—because he had lost all his property in the famous storm of June 1676 in Campeachy Bay. He had no money and no means of getting to Jamaica, and knew that if he fell into Spanish hands he would probably be enslaved for life. In these circumstances he and his few remaining companions hastened to take service with the first wandering buccaneer commander who came in sight.

Glancing through the list of the minor heroes of this time, Harris and Sharp and Cook, Cox and Sawkins—that sturdy Puritan who would not allow his men to gamble on Sundays—it is impossible to resist the conclusion that hardly any of them were pirates in the ordinary meaning of the word. They would have preferred a strictly legal profession and would have found it in any normal time. Ringrose, to whose narrative of Sharp's voyage we owe so much, Wafer, the surgeon, who lived for months among the Darien Indians, and many others like them, were decent, educated men. As for Dampier, he was by temperament and choice an explorer rather than a buccaneer, and proved it in his subsequent career. It was only a question of time, of course, before the English authorities joined with the Spanish in putting down all illegal trade; but in the meantime "privateering" was the obvious, always exciting, and often lucrative resort of every English out-of-work in the West Indies.

It is tempting to write many pages about that baffling, attractive character, William Dampier. He seems to me the very type of the romantic schoolboy who, without any natural gifts as a leader of men, but with an inborn passion for geography and for all strange sights, obstinately carved out for himself a career of adventure without parallel since the days of the Elizabethans. Always in some subordinate position he left one buccaneering ship after another, until he found a captain who was bound for the East Indies and so managed to sail all round the world. He landed in England after twelve years' absence, with no possessions except the clothes he stood up in, a half-share in a wretched, shivering tattooed native "prince" (who was exhibited at fairs all over England till he died of smallpox at Oxford) and the weather-stained sheets of his manuscript journal, which is still regarded to-day as one of the finest travel books in our language. I shall have more to say of him as an explorer later on.

Ringrose, Dampier's companion, was unfortunately killed at Santa Pecaque in 1686. Swan, that stout and flabby commander, had captured the town with an absurdly small following at the first assault, but had not the authority to keep his Englishmen out of the wine-cellars. In fact the buccaneers refused to move until all the booty had been carried down to their ships; so that Swan, against his better judgment, was compelled to send off a long string of pack-horses under a slender guard. Presently those in the town heard the sound of heavy firing. They still refused to move. Then came riderless horses, galloping in with blood-stained saddles.

Finally they sallied out, too late, and found the baggage train scattered and their comrades all dead. "They lay," says Dampier, "all along the path as they were killed, one and one, not two abreast anywhere, by which it was easy to guess that their own folly ruined them, for they had as many horses as men, and therefore every man led his horse, which made a great distance between the foremost and the hindermost, and the Spaniards had the advantage to destroy them singly." Among them was Basil Ringrose, Dampier's "ingenious friend," whose knowledge of Latin had often enabled him to act as interpreter between the Spaniards and the buccaneers. We get a fleeting picture of the dark-haired Dampier, with his melancholy, obstinate eyes standing grieving over the body of his friend by the side of the rough track near that South American city, so far from the little Somersetshire village which was his home. Ringrose was an honest and industrious chronicler, and the Spaniard who shot him down did an ill service to travel literature.

CHAPTER VII

THE GREAT NAVIGATORS IN THE SOUTH

WE have said that English exploration, if it did not exactly stand still, was at any rate marking time during the greater part of the seventeenth century. At the same time we have seen that both ship-building design and the study of navigation were rapidly improving towards the end of the century; and by 1713 that most useful and industrious of Royal Commissions, the Board of Longitude, had begun its sittings in London. It would almost seem that during this transition period English explorers, finding their activities curtailed by domestic turmoil, but with their appetite for discovery still unabated, were deliberately preparing themselves for the great effort which was to mark the middle years of the eighteenth century under the settled Hanoverian regime.

William Dampier forms the link between the two periods. He began as a seventeenth-century buccaneer, and ended as the eighteenth-century discoverer of the north-west coast of Australia. In the course of his voyage round the world with the buccaneers, he and his companions had paid a disappointingly casual kind of visit to Australia—"*Terra Australis Incognita*"—just "to see what that country would afford us." They were not impressed. The land (probably King Sound) was barren, and, as for the people, even the "Hodmadods" (Hottentots) though "a nasty people," were "gentlemen to these." The extraordinary thing about the Australian aboriginals was that even when taken on board the English ship they showed not the faintest interest in their surroundings (they can never have seen anything remotely resembling a three-masted double-decker in the whole of their lives), but merely grabbed at any food within reach. They could not even be tempted with mirrors, coloured cloths, or little pieces of finery—a point on which they showed themselves definitely inferior to monkeys.

In the seclusion of his Somersetshire village home, however, after his return to England, Dampier began to take a brighter view of the Australian adventure. As he said himself, it was not yet determined whether New Holland, as it was called, was an island or a "main continent." The Dutch, who had long been established in the Spice Islands to the north, had never taken the trouble to find out, for the Dutch were more interested in trade than in geography. There was a theory that Australia was really a continent but split in two by a wide waterway from west to east. Dampier thought it would be interesting to discover the truth; so he persuaded the Government to send him out in a King's ship, the *Roebuck*, carrying twelve guns and a crew of fifty men, and he set sail for Australia, *via* the Cape of Good Hope, in January 1699. Unfortunately he made for the north-western extremity of the continent and, having a crazy ship and a troublesome crew, and being prejudiced by a personal dislike of cold weather, he did not stay long enough to explore southward as far as the sites of the modern Perth and Fremantle nor pass the Straits of Torres and try the eastern side, which must have brought him to Queensland and Botany Bay. Instead he explored New Guinea and found the straits which now bear his name between New Guinea and New Britain. On the way home the *Roebuck* was lost at Ascension Island and Dampier had to face a court-martial. He subsequently made two further voyages round the world, once in command of the privateer *St. George*, and once as pilot to that very capable commander and entertaining writer, Woodes Rogers, of whom I shall have more to say. Dampier himself was one of the greatest of all English travel-writers. His easy, fluent style, his interest in everything he saw, and his remarkable powers of observation mark him off from the mere keepers of daily journals. Defoe owes much to him—more than he ever had the generosity to confess.

As an explorer, Dampier has generally been accounted a failure; but though he missed the plums himself, he undoubtedly showed the way for the great men who were to follow him. To attempt to record all the geographical discoveries of the eighteenth century would be an undertaking altogether outside the scope of this volume. We can only take a few names, as we have in previous centuries, and treat them as typical—and the two which at once spring to the mind are, of course, those of Anson and Cook. Though they were both of them employed in the service of their Government, no two men ever deserved better the title of adventurer. They were of very different types. Anson belonged to the professional classes, joined the Navy at the age of fifteen, and, after his famous voyage round the world, became a successful First Lord of the Admiralty. James Cook was a Yorkshireman, born of humble parentage, who ran away to sea as a boy and rose from the ranks. With his commanding presence and indomitable courage, he was a great leader of men, but we cannot picture him as an administrator. From the point of view of this book, it may be said that Anson was an adventurer by accident, whereas Cook was to the manner born. Anson, as we see him in his portraits, has the bland, confident look of an eighteenth-century man of affairs; Cook, with his knit eyebrows and his eager gaze apparently fixed on some far distant object, is the idealistic adventurer of all times.

Anson was born in 1697, the same year in which Dampier published his first account of his voyage round the world—a best-seller of those times. As a young officer, he was never in any important fleet action, but was engaged in convoy work and in punitive expeditions against the pirates—those decadent successors of the buccaneers—all of which tended to develop his natural gift of initiative. We may safely assume that Dampier's narratives were his favourite reading. On the outbreak of the Spanish War in 1737 he was given the command of the *Centurion*, of sixty guns, and a squadron of seven other vessels, with instructions to destroy Spanish shipping on the west coast of America and in the South Seas. Starting too late in the year (1740) he had a terrible passage round the Horn, losing most of his men by scurvy, and parting company with all the rest of his squadron. Nothing deterred, he refreshed his men at the island of Juan Fernandez, himself residing in a tent on shore, and then made a dashing and successful attack on the town of Payta on the mainland, where he captured much treasure. He then set out across the Pacific with his single remaining ship, the *Centurion*, intending to return to England, as other circumnavigators had done, *via* the Cape of Good Hope.

It was a rash enterprise for an officer in Anson's position, for in those days they did not prepare public banquets and newspaper eulogies for explorers who returned without their ships: they prepared courts-martial instead. But fortune favoured the brave. Anson, who had already enriched himself and his crew, had the extraordinary good luck to intercept the famous Spanish treasure galleon, the "Manila ship" on its way from Acapulco, in Mexico, to Manila Bay. The first Englishman who ever took this most celebrated of treasure-ships was Richard Cavendish, in the year 1587. Woodes Rogers repeated the feat in 1709. Anson was the third.

As he brought his own little ship under the quarter of the towering Spaniard, he saw that the enemy, though they had been specially warned of his presence in those waters, had only just begun to clear their decks for action by throwing over the cattle, the hen-coops, and other encumbrances. He immediately opened a brisk fire. The reduced ship's company on the *Centurion* was insufficient to supply crews for all the guns. So Anson appointed two men to remain with each gun and attend to the loading, while what may be called a firing party passed rapidly up and down the gun-decks discharging the weapons. The Spaniards, in their sea fights with the English, had learnt the habit of throwing themselves flat on the decks when they saw that a broadside was about to be discharged at them. But now the fire of the *Centurion* was continuous, giving no respite, and the enemy lost heavily (sixty-seven killed and eighty-four wounded) while their own reply was so feeble and ill-directed that only two men fell on the English ship. But it must not be thought that Anson's success was solely due to the imbecility of his opponent, for he got across the Spaniard's bows in very seamanlike style, raking her fore and aft, and managing his small armament in a manner which might well have defeated a worthier foe.

Just as the galleon struck her flag, one of Anson's lieutenants came to him and whispered that the *Centurion* was dangerously on fire near the powder room. Without moving a muscle of his face or allowing anyone to know what had happened, he calmly gave the necessary orders and the fire was extinguished just in time. Coolness in an emergency was one of Anson's leading characteristics. So was his iron discipline. There was something cold-blooded about him, something stiff-necked and official. But at the same time he could be very human and considerate in dealing with the humbler members of his crew. He took nearly £400,000 off the Manila ship and made them all rich for life. And when he returned to England, after encircling the globe, he was given a deservedly enthusiastic welcome. It was a great feat of arms.

Anson was poorly educated for a man of his class. He hated writing letters, was "awkward" in society (his own word), and never appeared at any kind of function if he could help it. As a London wit said of him, he had been round the world but never in it. To admirers of England's naval pageantry he may be recommended as the Lord of the Admiralty who instituted the first British naval uniform, the familiar blue and white in which his own portrait has been painted, and which Nelson wore. It is not generally realised that in the early part of the eighteenth century there was a serious danger that red would be generally adopted as the colour of the sea-officer's uniform, so that instead of our perfectly suitable navy blue the oceans of the world might have been speckled scarlet, as with measles. Anson averted that.

Cook was more than thirty years younger than Anson, but he never ceased adventuring—indeed, his life was one long adventure from the date when he gave his master the slip and went on board the collier at Whitby, to his murder in 1779 by hostile South Sea islanders. He was then fifty-one. Such a crowded career is impossible to summarise, and Cook's achievements were so many that it is difficult to pick out any one of them as typical. He was already twenty-seven when he joined the Navy, and he was over forty before he was given commissioned rank, having already distinguished himself as the master (or navigating officer) of several King's ships. He was then made a lieutenant in order that he might command the scientific expedition which was sent to the South Seas to study the transit of Venus in the year 1769. Having taken the necessary observations, he proceeded on the memorable voyage to Australia which resulted in the discovery of Botany Bay.

Up to a year or two ago it was commonly supposed that this voyage was an independent effort on Cook's part, undertaken by himself and his officers in a pure spirit of adventure, after a meeting in his cabin when the proposal was put to the vote and carried by a small majority. The discovery of the new continent had thus almost the appearance of an accident. In 1928, however, the Admiralty decided to release for publication their original copy of Cook's secret instructions, from which it plainly appears that Australia was always the real objective. The observation of the transit of Venus was mere camouflage, designed to conceal Cook's true destination from the jealous eyes of foreign nations —in particular France and Spain—with whom we were then on the edge of war.

The Lords of the Admiralty who signed these secret instructions (one of them was Admiral Brett, who as captain under Anson had led the storming party at Payta) were evidently agreed in doubting the existence of the great unknown southern continent, *Terra Australis Incognita*, which had been leading all the map-makers astray for the last three centuries. They believed that the only place where any new continent was likely to be found was where Cook did, in fact, find it. They further held that "the making discoveries of countries hitherto unknown and the attaining of a knowledge of distant parts which, though formerly discovered, have yet been imperfectly explored, will redound greatly to the honour of this nation as a Maritime Power, as well as to the dignity of the Crown of Great Britain, and may tend greatly to the advancement of the trade and navigation thereof."

In appointing James Cook they had chosen the right man to translate this fine ambition into fact. When he left New Zealand to sail westward into the unknown he had a bare six months' provisions on board the *Endeavour*, and his sails and rigging were showing the effect of nineteen months at sea. Yet so far was he from being content with the mere discovery of New South Wales, which in itself assured his fame for all time, that he proceeded to chart the whole eastern coast of Australia from end to end and to take possession of a continent in the name of his King. It was characteristic of him that he would never leave any task until he had completed it to his entire satisfaction. The great French navigator, La Perouse, when he was off the coast of Australia eighteen years later, remarked to an English officer: "Mr. Cook has done so much that he has left me nothing to do but to admire his works."

It is true, of course, that Cook's ship, the *Endeavour*, was infinitely better built and rigged than, for instance, Dampier's *Roebuck*; the difference between the *Roebuck* and the *Endeavour* was very much greater than between the *Endeavour* and a ship of Nelson's time. Crews were still collected in the old careless way: many of them were landsmen, and in time of war (though this would not apply to Cook's ships) the press-gangs and the debtors' prisons would supply any deficiency in numbers. Discipline would be as strict as ever, and Cook was nothing if not a disciplinarian. At the same time he was one of the first sea-captains to take an intelligent interest in the question of dietary. He fed his crews well and understood the importance of fresh food if scurvy was to be avoided. In his first voyage to Australia he did not lose a single man by sickness. Without a wonderfully clean bill of health, he could never have remained six months surveying and mapping on the Australian coast and carried his ship back to England. He was a benevolent despot on board ship, a big, solemn, almost godlike personage. He never had to quell a mutiny, as Drake, and Magellan, and Christopher Columbus did. If quarrels broke out among his men he rode the tempest with the same massive ease and dignity with which the figure-head of his vessel breasted the waves.

One year after his discovery of modern Australia, Cook was sent out again, now with captain's rank, in command of the ship *Resolution* of 462 tons, with a smaller vessel in company, with orders to solve finally the age-long puzzle of *Terra Australis Incognita*, the mythical southern continent which was supposed to stretch away from somewhere south of Australia to the Antarctic polar regions. For several weeks he sailed to and fro over latitudes marked in most maps of his time as solid land, and returned to

England with another great, if negative, achievement to his credit. In 1776 he sailed on his last
voyage, the object of which was to search for the
North-west Passage between the Pacific and the
Atlantic—that most ancient lure of mariners—but
approaching it for the first time from the Pacific
side. Cook, on his way out, discovered group after
group of the South Sea Islands never yet sighted by
Europeans—in fact he re-mapped the Pacific; and
after an unsuccessful attempt to penetrate the
Behring Straits, he put back to Hawaii to winter.
It was here that he met his cruel death in February
1779.

There had been some trouble with the natives.
One of the ship's boats was stolen, not because the
natives would make any use of the boat, but because
they wanted the nails with which its planks were
held together, to turn them into fish hooks. This
was a serious loss. Cook followed his usual method
on such occasions, which was to secure the person
of the king and hold him as a hostage until the
culprits were given up. As his second-in-command
was ill, he personally went ashore for this purpose,
and had got the frightened and indignant king down
on to the beach, when a rumour spread among the
natives that one of their chiefs had been killed by a
shot fired from an English boat.

This was, unfortunately, true. The boats were
stretched in a cordon across the bay to prevent the
natives from escaping in their canoes while the
question of the stolen cutter was still in dispute.
One of the English boats, commanded by an
officer named Bligh (of whom we shall presently

hear more), perceiving a native canoe apparently attempting to run the blockade, opened fire, and at the first discharge unluckily killed a leading chief who was well known to be a friend of the English.

When this news reached the beach, the islanders were stirred to madness and pressed upon Cook and the officer who was with him, threatening them with their weapons. The king was allowed to escape, but the attitude of the crowd was as menacing as ever, and the English officers could with difficulty keep them at bay. They were walking slowly backwards and had almost reached the water's edge, when the men in the boat, seeing their peril, began to discharge their muskets into the midst of the pursuing crowd. This was contrary to all Cook's ideas. It meant that friendly relations with this people would be interrupted, perhaps for years. Without thinking of his own danger, he turned round towards the boats and raised his arms as a signal to cease fire. At the same moment he was both bludgeoned and stabbed from behind, and fell on his face in the surf where the savages soon made an end of him.

A year later occurred the celebrated mutiny of the *Bounty*. No adventure of the seas has attracted more attention in recent years. The ship was engaged to fetch specimens of the breadfruit tree from the South Seas to the West Indies, with the idea of growing it in the latter place, and establishing a trade with Europe. She had visited many of the islands discovered by Cook, where the natives had inquired eagerly after him, for he always had the trick of winning their affection and trust. Early on the morning of 28th August 1789, the commander

of the *Bounty*, William Bligh, was roughly awakened
to find himself looking down the barrels of muskets
held by mutinous members of his crew, while their
ringleader, a midshipman named Christian, whom
Bligh had alternately pampered and bullied (for he
was a thoroughly bad commander) was threatening
him with a cutlass.

The scene that followed is too well known to need
more than a brief description here. Bligh was
dragged on deck in his white ruffled shirt, and his
eighteenth-century knee-breeches, with his hands
tied behind him so tightly as to cause him great
pain. A boat was hoisted out, and he was thrust
into it, with eighteen loyal members of the crew
after him. The boatswain, who was among them,
managed to secure a quadrant and compass, with a
cask of water, some bread and some rum. As the
boat drifted clear under the *Bounty's* stern, there was
an extraordinary scene between the two parties
which has been immortalised in a well-known
painting. Bligh, who with all his faults never lacked
courage, continued to appeal to the mutineers to
return to their duty, and some of the carpenters
from the lower stern windows shouted to him that
they were detained against their will. Other
sympathisers threw out to the boat a few pieces of
pork, some clothes, and four cutlasses (their only
weapons). Christian, for his part, as he glared down
at them from the poop, had nothing but curses to
give them, and seemed to regret that he had left one
of them alive.

We need not follow in any detail the subsequent
movements of the mutineers; how they drifted

about from place to place, and finally took native wives and settled on Pitcairn Island, where their descendants may be seen to this day, and where that strange temperamental Manxman, Fletcher Christian, met his end. The greater adventure belongs to Bligh. This blustering bully and martinet, finding himself with eighteen helpless people (for all the best seamen were among the mutineers) in an open boat, thousands of miles from a friendly port, suddenly developed powers of leadership which have won him a well-deserved place in history. Desperate, half-starving, they made their way slowly across the Pacific, first one and then another dropping from fatigue, Bligh alone despising every hardship. He reached Australia, wriggled through the Great Barrier Reef (the passage is still named after him), past the Straits of Torres, and finally arrived at Timor with the survivors of his party after a voyage of about four thousand miles. His own cool account of this journey, with its daily record of hairbreadth escapes and hardships almost beyond belief, makes one of the best tales of adventure in our language.

Bligh afterwards served at Camperdown, and also at Copenhagen where his ship was next in line to Nelson's and he was personally thanked by the Admiral on the latter's quarter-deck. His last post was that of Governor of the new convict settlement in New South Wales, where his methods of discipline provoked one of the most serious revolts in the history of the Colony. He died in London two years after Waterloo—an unpleasant character, with one noble achievement to his credit.

One other great name must be mentioned before

we leave Australia and the Southern Seas—that of Matthew Flinders. In company with the naval surgeon, George Bass, he sailed round Tasmania in 1798, a hazardous voyage, in a small boat, and, by the discovery of Bass Straits proved that the island was not part of the mainland, as Cook had supposed. Later he explored the extreme southern coast of Australia, which had been left out by Cook, and finally circumnavigated the whole continent in 1803, charting the seas and noting the lie of the land with a thoroughness worthy of his great predecessor. Indeed he left little more to be done in that part of the world, the discovery and exploration of which has formed the chief subject of this chapter. There were to be many more English adventurers in Australia and the South Seas; there are many there to-day. But the work of the great pioneers—of the men who sailed out into the "blue" looking for undiscovered islands and continents on the other side of the world, and lay off those far distant beaches in their boats, calmly tossing ashore beads and mirrors and other trinkets at the feet of the mobs of black savages who howled and shook their weapons in reply—the work of these men was done. The clouds of ignorance and of a too fertile imagination had rolled away, taking with them not only the headless men, the dragons spitting fire, and the wild pigs with their navels in the middle of their backs, but a whole southern continent of vast extent which had figured on the map for centuries; while new islands innumerable, and even a new continent, the existence of which had only been guessed at, had arisen out of the sea as if by magic to take their place.

CHAPTER VIII

PRIVATEERS AND SOLDIERS OF FORTUNE

SURVEYING the crowded canvas of the eighteenth century for the purposes of such a book as this, perhaps the leading fact that springs to the eye, and leaves one wondering why it has been so little emphasised before, is the amazing *variety* of the period. In an age of lace and ruffles, powder and patches, and a charming artificiality which the nineteenth century despised but we are able to admire, it is startling to encounter the bluff countenance of an admiral of the fleet, the dry features of an Indian nabob, or to read of the rough, open-air life of the vast majority of the population. Horace Walpole and Captain Cook, Casanova and the Vicar of Wakefield, John Wesley and Captain Kidd are all of this prolific century.

The reader must not therefore be shocked by a rather abrupt change of scene. In our last chapter we breathed the pure and rarefied atmosphere of disinterested scientific research. The great navigators who were our heroes sought only to increase the sum of human knowledge and asked for no reward but glory. It would indeed have taken a brave man to suggest any lower motive in the dignified presence of an Anson or a Cook. Yet it would be putting it mildly to say that ninety-nine per cent. of the adventurers of the eighteenth century put out to sea, or set forth upon some inland voyage, with no thought at all of science in their minds.

We have been speaking of the sea, so may begin now upon the sailors—men who had absolutely nothing in common with Cook and Anson except their adventurousness. The mere number of them daunts the historian. They carried the new Union Jack of Great Britain over every sea and into every clime, and committed every kind of sin and every sort of heroism beneath its shadow. Mentally assembling just a few of their names, one feels like a man confronted by an immense pile of bricks and told to build a house with them. Indeed the architecture of this chapter is so difficult that the best plan will probably be to give the problem up altogether, and merely walk cursorily through the century, selecting an outstanding figure here and there from the crowded ranks of these unofficial adventurers by sea.

Why not, therefore, begin with Woodes Rogers, that debonair and charming commander? We have already mentioned him as one of the three Englishmen who had the honour of capturing a Manila treasure-ship. But he was no mere filibuster. He would not attack a Spanish ship unless England and Spain were at war. His career marks the change from the seventeenth-century buccaneer to the eighteenth-century privateer. And it is interesting to note that when he started off from Bristol (for he was a Bristol man) on his remarkably successful voyage round the world (1708-1711) he had with him as pilot William Dampier, who was a man of both periods, a kind of connecting link.

Just a word about privateers. A privateer is a private person who puts to sea with an authorisation from his own Government to "annoy the King's enemies" (to quote the oldest licences, which go back as far as the reign of Henry III) and is therefore entitled, in the event of his capture, to be treated as a combatant and accorded the usual courtesies of war. In the Middle Ages these licences or "letters of marque" were of two kinds—those which were granted to an ordinary adventurer who was out to get what he could and share the proceeds with the Government, and those which were granted to some merchant who, having been robbed by the enemy, was now authorised to take from them, if he could, goods to the same value. But this second type of privateer had disappeared long before the opening of the eighteenth century. The men we are now dealing with knew no limit upon the amount of their booty, except the capacity of the ship's hold; and the British Government, as we shall see, sought to encourage their activities by constantly reducing its own claims, until towards the end of the century a privateer commander, his owners and his crew, were allowed to divide among themselves almost everything they had gained.

Woodes Rogers set sail at a time when ships were not easy to man for a long voyage, and when the general ignorance of geography was such that crews were often terrified (as Dampier relates) at being taken across the Pacific lest they should sail clean out of the world! In Woodes Rogers's two

ships, the *Duke* and *Duchess*, most of the men were
land-lubbers, and none was properly dressed, for
he had not dared to admit to them his intention of
encircling the globe. When he got to Madeira he
confessed the truth, and describes in his own breezy,
inimitable style how he offered them the choice of
obtaining new, warm clothing for the cold weather
round the Horn, or a supply of that island's generous
wines. Without one dissentient vote they elected
to be warmed inside rather than out.

The voyage continued. Wherever he went
Woodes Rogers made friends with the local Spanish
or Portuguese governors, for he had a wonderful
way with him. At the Portuguese island of Grande,
off the Brazilian coast, the English were invited to
join in a religious procession through the town, it
being a saint's day, and took their ship's band ashore
for the purpose. First came the musicians, then "an
old Father and two Fryars carrying Lamps of
Insence," then the sacred images, then the Governor,
with Woodes Rogers and his officers solemnly
carrying lighted candles, then the principal inhabitants, and other priests. The bandsmen who, as
Woodes Rogers tells us, were by this time more than
half drunk, played "Hey boys, up go we," and "all
manner of noisy paltry tunes." However, the
Portuguese never knew the difference, and the whole
ceremony went off very well and cordially.

Rounding the "Cape of Storms" in freezing
weather and thanking God for their Madeira they
arrived at last, one evening, off the island of Juan
Fernandez where it was proposed to wait and rest.
As the *Duke's* boat pushed in towards the shore,

there was a wild half-naked figure running up and down the beach waving a white rag! While they sought for a convenient landing-place, he shouted instructions in a strange stumbling voice which none of them could understand. This was Alexander Selkirk, the Scottish cobbler's son, who had been marooned there four and a half years before at his own request (having quarrelled with his shipmates until he could not stand the sight of them another minute) and was now to spring into fame as Defoe's model for *Robinson Crusoe*. Selkirk had learned to run so fast that he beat the ship's bulldog every time. Strangest of all he had quite lost his taste for rum and brandy. They made him mate of the *Duchess* and, after a pleasant rest on this most celebrated of desert islands, started north again, and on 22nd December 1709 had the extraordinary good fortune to capture one of the Manila treasure-ships. There was a brisk engagement before the Spaniard struck, and Woodes Rogers was shot through the jaw and badly wounded; but he remained on deck delivering his orders in writing, since he could not speak.

An attempt to capture a second Manila ship was repulsed by the Spaniards, but Woodes Rogers and his merry men were already rich, and when they eventually got back to England, on 1st October 1711, having crossed the Pacific and circumnavigated the globe, they had so valuable a cargo on board that the net profits of the voyage amounted to nearly £800,000—an enormous sum in those days. This was the real significance of the voyage—that it was so successful and (perhaps even more important) that its success had been attained with such an appearance of ease. Woodes Rogers's geniality and personal courage had endeared him to the men, while the many experienced officers under his command had been flattered by being taken into his confidence at every step. In England it was realised for the first time that it was possible to sail all round the world, under the right kind of commander, and bring back all your ships and most of your men fit and well, and with their pockets bulging with gold. The example of Woodes Rogers was quickly followed, and, though none of his imitators did quite as well as he did, the idea of a long sea voyage had now lost many of its terrors.

George Shelvocke circumnavigated the globe in 1719-1722. He held a commission from King George to "cruise on the Spaniards," but often behaved more like a pirate than a privateer. His officers were unsatisfactory, and his men were always on the verge of mutiny. The most celebrated incident of the voyage was the appearance of a huge black albatross, which followed the ship for days, until Hatley, one of the officers, taking it for a portent of evil, seized a gun and shot it down. Seventy-six years later Wordsworth read Shelvocke's account of his voyage, and, coming upon this story, suggested it to Coleridge as a good subject for a poem, and Coleridge wrote *The Ancient Mariner*.

Shelvocke died in 1742. In 1739 had broken out the War of Jenkins's Ear, which interrupted Walpole's long peace. We now approach the greatest period in the history of privateering. It is obvious

that when the Navy was performing its duties
efficiently, destroying enemy commerce and retain-
ing command of the sea, the privateer became
unnecessary and even undesirable. Nelson, for
instance, regarded privateers as little better than
pirates and was in favour of doing away with them
altogether, and that was the common view of the
naval officer, and of the general public too, at every
period in our history when the King's ships were
capable of doing everything that the privateer set
forth to do without his assistance. At such times
the privateer was a mere jackal to the fleet, a hanger-
on, a picker-up of unconsidered trifles, and his
character and appearance kept pace with his moral
decline.

But at the time we are now considering—a
period of about twenty years in the middle of the
eighteenth century—the British Navy was at its
worst. Corruption was rampant—though that was
nothing new, for bribery was the rule throughout
the public services, from the Prime Minister down-
wards; but charges of slackness and even cowardice
in the face of the enemy were a strange and unpleasant feature in our naval annals. Yet accusations
of the kind were at this time freely bandied about in
Parliament, laughed over in the coffee-houses and
printed in the newspapers. As a modern critic
remarks[1]: "It almost seems to the student, wading
among this garbage, as if nothing important ever
happened for many years without somebody being
court-martialled." And it was towards the end of
this unhappy period (in 1757 to be precise) that a

[1] Mr. H. S. Vaughan.

French visitor to one of our naval ports was startled to observe a grim little ceremony taking place upon the quarter deck of the flagship. A stout middle-aged gentleman with a handkerchief over his eyes confronted a row of red-coated marines. A chaplain said a few words to him and retired. There was a hoarse word of command, a volley rang out, and the stout gentleman fell dead. The visitor, much shocked, applied to his English guide for information. He was told that the victim was Admiral Byng, who had failed to bring a French fleet to action. "But," objected the visitor, "the French admiral seems to have been equally pusillanimous." "That may be so," replied the guide, "but in this country we find it necessary to shoot an admiral from time to time *pour encourager les autres.*"

And the truth is that it *did* encourage them: at any rate, the date of Byng's death may be said to mark, roughly, the end of this dismal period in our naval history. In the meantime the privateer captain had seized his opportunity and reached the pinnacle of his fame. Men like Commodore Walker, Fortunatus Wright, William Hutchinson, and Captain Phillips, were capable, patriotic commanders who did at least as much for the honour of England on the high seas as any naval officer of that time. And since on a privateer the discipline was easier, the food better, and the financial rewards much greater than on a man-of-war, it is not surprising to find that they easily manned their ships without the help of a press-gang, and that one of the daily problems for the harbour authorities was to prevent sailors from deserting from the King's ships to the privateers.

Commodore Walker, of whose varied career we have a lively account, tells an excellent story of how a rival privateer at Exeter seduced the crew of Walker's ship, then lying at Dartmouth, by the simple process of offering them three guineas each to join him. Walker pursued his men in a post-chaise along the dusty road from Dartmouth to Exeter, and came up with them near the gates of the latter city. He reproached them bitterly, whereupon their leader stepped forward, and hitching up his trousers, no doubt, and pulling his forelock in the traditional manner, explained that they never meant to desert, but had designed to have a laugh at the expense of Walker's Exeter rival by taking his bribes and then returning to Dartmouth. "By God," added the honest fellow, "we are men of strict honour, but we love money and a joke, the two best things in the world next to a whore and fighting." There you have the philosophy of the eighteenth-century privateer!

It was no idle boast to say they liked fighting. Only once in his career did Walker have to deal with a mutiny, and that was when his crew wanted him to attack a Dutch ship, upon some rumour that she was a Frenchman in disguise. Walker's toughest fights were with the French, but his most resounding exploit was the capture of the Spanish seventy-four the *Glorioso*. This warship was being used for the transport of treasure from America, and Walker probably knew it. Otherwise it is hard to believe that he would have tackled a line-of-battle ship. Privateersmen were usually paid no regular wages; they looked for their livelihood to the capture of rich prizes, and naturally they preferred an ill-armed merchantman to a man-of-war. Like lonely wolves they prowled over all the oceans of the world looking for any fat trader whom their letters of marque might authorise them to attack. The empty glory of a successful action against a frigate or an armed brig made no appeal to them. But any ship with a cargo was fair game, and if the cargo happened to be on a battleship they were not the men to hold back. Both their greed and their indisputable courage drove them on.

Walker overhauled the *Glorioso* in his little *King George* of only thirty guns. Following him were other English ships of about the same size; but just as the *King George* began to engage the big Spaniard, yard-arm to yard-arm, the wind dropped to a dead calm so that there was nothing to do but to make the best of an unequal duel. The action began at eight o'clock "on a clear moonshine evening." Walker's ship was much belaboured. The Portuguese fort on Cape St. Vincent, observing this action, which was taking place very irregularly in neutral waters, attempted to keep the peace—or perhaps merely to re-affirm Portuguese neutrality—by opening fire upon the combatants—and the poor little *King George*, being the nearer of the two, got most of these attentions. After two and a half hours the wind freshened and, one of Walker's consorts coming up, the *Glorioso* made off. But two English warships suddenly appeared from the westward and headed her off, and the rest of the privateers getting under weigh she was surrounded and captured after a gallant resistance. In the midst of the engagement one of the King's ships, the *Dartmouth*, suddenly blew up. Among the few survivors of her crew who were picked up was a solitary officer, an Irish midshipman named O'Brien. "Sir," he said to the English privateer commander who rescued him, "you must excuse the unfitness of my dress to come aboard a strange ship, but really I left my own in such a hurry that I had no time to stay for a change." "A young gentleman of great ease in behaviour," comments Walker admiringly, "and of a happy readiness of wit." We are reminded of Midshipman Easy and of the fact that another of Marryat's heroes was an Irish middy named O'Brien.

With that we may say good-bye to the privateers. The sound of their puny artillery was soon to be lost in the thunder of the Napoleonic wars. In that great earth-shaking conflict there was little room for the private adventurer as such. Certain frigate captains were at times enabled to lead a sort of free-lance existence, preying upon enemy commerce and waxing fat on prize money—to the indignation of line-of-battle captains in the fleet. The greatest of these was Lord Cochrane—an excitable sailor of the true adventurous, undisciplined type. He quarrelled with every one, and was always both a genius and a nuisance. With his first command, a tiny brig, mounting fourteen four-pounders, he took no less than fifty prizes, including a Spanish frigate of thirty-two guns, and finally surrendered to three French ships-of-the-line after a long and vigorous resistance. But Lord St. Vincent, that stern old disciplinarian, could not stand him, and so he missed Trafalgar and much else besides, and, after being struck off the Navy list went and offered his services to Chile and led that republic's preposterous little fleet from victory to victory, in a manner which has never yet been explained. Quarrelling with the Government of Chile, he offered his services to the Brazilian patriots and helped them mightily in their struggle to free themselves from Portugal. On one occasion, with his single ship, he chased a squadron of thirteen Portuguese men-of-war all the way from Bahia to Lisbon, capturing or driving ashore most of the transports they were escorting. On another, after an unusually successful cruise, when some church furniture was included among the booty, he brought his frigate into port with a five-foot golden candlestick glittering at each masthead. Quarrelling with the Brazilians in their turn, he went to Greece, took command of the Greek Navy, and retained the post until the nation had won its independence. But by that time Byron and Trelawney and a dozen other adventurers were there. In fact we have reached the year 1829 and are stumbling blindly into our next chapter.

To return to the land. At the opening of the eighteenth century the whole appearance of English society was considerably affected by a fact which has not always been sufficiently emphasised in this connection—namely that a new kind of adventurous career with the possibility of great financial rewards now offered itself to the younger sons of the nobility and, indeed, to any enterprising youth of the better classes. This was what may be called the colonial career, and it was quite a new feature in English life. It was not a question of flying from

home to avoid religious persecution or imprison-
ment, and founding a family in the wilds of America;
it was a question of a long exile among the ancient
countries of the East, with the object always in mind
of accumulating enough money to return to England
in your old age. For most Englishmen it meant
India. There was eager competition for quite poorly
paid posts in the service of the East India Company;
and there were plenty of "interlopers" who sailed
east to trade on their own account in defiance of the
Company's monopoly. The returned Indian nabob,
with his parchment skin, his swarthy servants, his
ridiculous personal habits and his incredible wealth,
appears for the first time in Piccadilly, to the vast
amusement of the young Whig exquisites of the
period, who were never quite sure which type they
despised most, a nabob, an admiral who had lost a
leg in battle, or a fox-hunting country squire.

Yet the story of the nabob's career, if they could
have brought themselves to listen to him, must
surely have stirred even their limited imaginations.
Let us take as an example—Thomas Pitt, or "Diamond" Pitt as he was called, the grandfather of the
great Earl of Chatham. Pitt went to sea in his teens,
and at the age of twenty-two was doing so well as
an "interloper" or independent trader in India that
the Company sent out peremptory orders to arrest
and imprison him. But he had already sailed for
Persia, where again he was extraordinarily successful. Returning to India, he continued to accumulate
wealth and avoid arrest by methods of extreme
caution alternating with sudden bold strokes — a
style peculiar to him. Finally the Company capitu-

lated and made him President of Fort St. George, in which position he soon made things unpleasant for his former associates, the "interlopers." Unfortunately Pitt had a bitter tongue, and in 1709, after a succession of disputes with his colleagues and the Company, he threw up his post and returned to England, bringing with him the enormous diamond, weighing 410 carats in the rough, from which he got his nickname. It had been stolen by an English skipper from a slave who found it in the Parteal mines on the Kistna and had hidden it in a wound in his leg.

The life of an Englishman in the East in those days is vividly described in Alexander Hamilton's *New Account of the East Indies* (1688-1723). Almost all our knowledge of the ports and coasting trade of the East in the early eighteenth century comes from his crowded but entertaining pages. He also was an "interloper," and he also was eventually "bought out" by the East India Company. But any rival skipper against whom he bore a grudge would fly from the sight of Hamilton's ship as from a pirate. Once when he was off Singapore the Sultan of Johore sent on board for a boy slave who had run away and hidden on the English ship. Hamilton pitched the royal messenger overboard. Apparently the Sultan liked him all the better for this, for he offered him Singapore (then an insignificant spot) as a free gift in perpetuity. Hamilton refused it! We owe much to this sturdy adventurer for his admirable description of the East Indies at the time when they were just becoming familiar to Englishmen.

It would be idle to deny that these early nabobs

had certain faults of temperament. They were extremely irascible, hectoring in their manner, impatient of argument, headstrong in action, greedy and avaricious; they drank too much sherry and Madeira and liked their curries red-hot. The type persisted throughout the century, was immortalised by Dickens in Major Bagstock, and continues, if only as a tradition, even to-day. Yet there was a special quality about them which can hardly escape the attention of the most casual reader of the lives of our adventurers. There was something Irish in their temper, a kind of divine madness, varied by fits of cold and calculated cunning. And it is perhaps more than a coincidence that the greatest of them all, of whom we must now say a few words, was an Irishman.

George Thomas was born in Tipperary of obscure parentage in 1756. He ran away to sea, deserted his ship in India, turned up at Hyderabad, where he enlisted as a private in the army of Nizam Ali Khan, tired of this employment, and walked on foot—an ignorant Irish cabin-boy!—all the thousand miles to Delhi, through a country then in a state of perpetual civil war with robber bands lurking near every high road. He joined the army of the Begum Somru, composed of regular troops, and soon rose to be commander-in-chief. It is impossible to describe the rest of his amazing career in any detail. Having quarrelled with his employer, he found himself with a band of desperadoes who would follow him anywhere, but with no money for their wages. He therefore stormed the nearest town, replenished his coffers, and from that time may be ranked as a leader of mercenaries, in direct descent from Knollys and Hawkwood.

It was an astonishing period in Indian history. There was something heroic about it, dating back to Homer rather than Hawkwood. In addition to Thomas and other military adventurers operating in Hindustan, "innumerable European free-lances served the courts of Hyderabad and Mysore and other native princes in southern India."[1] They overturned dynasties and ruled provinces at their will. They were not all Englishmen; for as the French power declined, French officers took more and more to this roving life. De Boigne created for Madhoji Sindhia the first complete army of regular troops employed by an Indian ruler. He was succeeded in the command by Perron, whose native battalions were for long irresistible against all but European troops. In the end Lord Wellesley broke up these gallant French brigades; but, in the meantime, English officers were often found fighting on opposing sides in the native wars. At the battle of Poonah in 1802, between Jaswant Rao Holkar and Sindhia, a gallant young Englishman was killed while leading a charge of Holkar's infantry against Sindhia's guns, which were commanded by another Englishman, Captain Dawes. Dawes also was killed in this battle. It is a lively page in the history of English adventure which is not read to-day as it deserves to be.

But though Englishmen fought on both sides, they never forgot their loyalty to their own flag.

---

[1] *A Particular Account of the European Military Adventurers*, by Herbert E. Compton. London, 1892.

When war broke out between Holkar and the British in 1804, three young officers in Holkar's service, Dodd, Ryan, and Vickers (who was a half-caste) were asked if they would fight against their countrymen. They refused, and were shortly afterwards executed and their heads stuck up on lances outside the camp. Like De Boigne and Perron, these English adventurers seem always to have used what influence they possessed in the interest of their own country.

Meantime George Thomas, our wild Irishman, had been getting into trouble with every one, and had set up an independent principality of his own, with his own arms factories, and was even contemplating the conquest of the Punjab for King George. But Sindhia's vastly superior forces, commanded by Perron's successor, Bergouin, surrounded him and forced him to surrender. The European officers in the besieging force courteously invited their prisoner to dinner in a big marquee. Wine flowed freely, and Thomas, as usual, got drunk. Some tactless idiot proposed a toast to the success of "Perron's brigades." The Irishman sprang to his feet with inflamed countenance, and drawing his sword soon cleared a space around him. "One Irish sword," he yelled triumphantly, as the tent emptied, "is still sufficient for a hundred Frenchmen!" But Captain Skinner and other Englishmen serving with Bergouin crowded round him and induced him to go home. Arriving at his own camp he was challenged by a sentry, and immediately slashed out at the unfortunate sepoy, cutting off his hand.

His career was finished, and he knew it. He set out for Calcutta with his half-caste family, but died on the way, some say of drink, more likely of a broken heart. He was a huge fellow physically, a man of vision in a political sense, an expert in the military art (particularly in military engineering), and possessed of an irresistible berserk courage. At the battle of Fatehpur, Thomas with no more than two thousand men defeated in the open field an army of forty thousand well supplied with artillery. He was called the "Scourge of the Sikhs," whose women used to frighten naughty children with the dreaded name of " Jowruj Jung." In his principality of Hariana he is said to have minted his own rupees. He fought and drank like a viking.

CHAPTER IX

LETTING LIGHT INTO AFRICA

WITH the discovery and colonisation of America and Australia, and the establishment of a regular trade with all the great nations of the East, both by sea and by the caravan routes of the interior, there remained only one of the five continents—Africa—which still offered to European adventurers the prospect of exploration on the grand scale—the discovery of the unknown, the turning of wild myth and conjecture into scientific fact. On the northern coast of Africa, bordering upon the Mediterranean, were the longest discovered countries in the world, and, in that sense, the best known. Here was Egypt, the cradle of our civilisation, which was already carefully mapped two thousand years before any civilised man set foot in England. Even at the opening of the nineteenth century its geography was better known than that of Russia. It had been one of the battlegrounds of the Napoleonic wars. But all the rest of that vast continent, save for a few Dutch and Portuguese settlements and a fort here and there at the mouths of the rivers, was veiled in a mystery more impenetrable than that which shrouded China before Marco Polo's journeys. No one even attempted to guess at what lay beyond the dark forests or the bold, imposing mountain ranges which bounded the horizon.

The typical travellers' tales of Asia and America, of misshapen men and gigantic women and impossibly horrible beasts, were curiously lacking in the case of Africa. Africa was an admitted mystery. Even the Arab slave-dealers, who were there long before us, and—with a hardihood we cannot but admire—made considerable journeys into the interior for their "black ivory," had little to tell. For they hurried by the shortest route from place to place, never leaving the beaten track, nor turning aside at any stealthy sound among the bushes or a glimpse of the whites of black men's eyes staring at them from some dim, festering swamp. No one pretended to know anything about Africa. The Dark Continent the nineteenth century named it, not inaptly. It was the great feat of the century to let in light upon this darkness, so that nowadays it is only in the very heart of the continent that the natives have not heard of gin and bowler hats, and regulations have to be passed to prevent wealthy American tourists from shooting down all the remaining elephants or chasing the lions off their feet with motor cars.

But the explorer of the nineteenth century, like his predecessors of the sixteenth and eighteenth, needed some incentive, some definite goal to aim at. This time the lure was the discovery of the sources of the Nile and the Niger. The former river, upon which the oldest and the most thickly populated country in the world depended for its prosperity, and indeed for its very existence, had never been traced back to its sources, which were a mere matter of legend to the decadent descendants of the Pharaohs.

But an eighteenth century Englishman named Bruce, a tall, handsome young fellow, six feet four inches in height, had travelled to Cosseir *via* Cairo in 1768, and, after carefully charting the Red Sea, had sailed south to Abyssinia, penetrated to the capital town, which was then Gondar, discovered the source of the *Blue* Nile among the Abyssinian hills, and returned to Egypt through the Sudan. So that little now remained to do, so far as could be seen by a generation which had not learnt to differentiate between the Blue Nile and the White. Bruce, who had suffered appalling hardships in the desert, being several times left for dead, met his death in a rather curious way in 1794. He was hurrying to help an old lady downstairs, when he slipped and fell on his head. He died a disappointed man, for no one would believe his stories of black men who wore rings in their lips and not in their ears, and thought it decorative to hang the entrails of animals around their necks; and when, in disgust, he retired (being then only forty-four) to his estate in Kinnaird, and solaced himself with experiments in astronomy, the natives merely concluded that the Laird was "gaen daft."

About this time the African Association was founded, a typical eighteenth century organisation, full of energy and vision, and with that wonderful gift, apparently peculiar to that century, of never holding a meeting without getting something done. After Bruce's death the Association, supposing the mystery of the Nile to be solved, turned its attention to the Niger. First it sent out Major David Houghton, who started from Gambia for the Niger's source, but wandered too far north, was captured by Moors, stripped naked and left to die in the desert. That might have been the end of the matter in a less adventurous age; but almost immediately a young Scottish ship's surgeon named Mungo Park volunteered to make a second attempt and started out, also from Gambia, in 1795.

When the streets of Paris were running red with blood and politicians were raving about liberty, equality, and fraternity, and Jacobin clubs were being formed even in England, and Europe was hurriedly arming itself against this new, truculent bolshevism, there was still a sufficient number of genuine adventurers whose thoughts were far away upon the deep bosoms of those mighty rivers of Africa whose sources were yet waiting to be found. While the tumbrils rattled over the cobblestones to the Place de la Révolution loaded with people who had risked their all on some political difference, or, more likely, in a bitter personal intrigue, Houghton and Park and others like them were taking their lives in their hands in a spirit of disinterested adventure, with the hope that they might add something definite to the sum total of human knowledge.

Mungo Park came in sight of the Niger on 20th July 1796. He also had suffered on the way; but his worst troubles began after he had reached his goal. As he made his way back, he was robbed and stripped as Houghton was; but one of the thieves, more humane than the rest, turned back and gave him his shirt, breeches and hat (in the crown of which he kept his diaries). As he lay on the ground in despair after the robbers had gone, his gallant spirit almost broken at last, he noticed a small patch of moss growing without any apparent means of sustenance on the side of a rock. If God could so miraculously preserve this moss, he thought, there might still be a chance for Mungo Park; and he rose and staggered on to the nearest native town, where the king was exceptionally cordial and not only fed him, but sent after the thieves and recovered his horse and baggage. His money was now finished, but he found a friendly slave-dealer who was taking slaves to the West Coast to sell to the English, and with this dismal train he performed the remainder of his return journey. He reached England in 1797.

Mungo Park attempted to settle down as a country doctor at Peebles, and he formed a close friendship with the great Sir Walter Scott. But his heart was always in Africa, and in 1805 (the year of Trafalgar) he started out again, this time with the "fixed resolution to discover the termination of the Niger or perish in the attempt." He led a party of forty men, thirty-five of them soldiers. There are many occasions when no one could ask for a better companion or a stauncher comrade than a British soldier, but not on an expedition into the wilds of Africa— not on an occasion requiring adaptability, patience, temperance, rather than courage and the spirit of devil-may-care. When they reached the Niger there were only eleven soldiers left, including their officer, Lieutenant Martyn. And when they had built a boat for the purpose of further exploration and had started off down the river, after sending Park's diaries home in charge of a Mandingo guide, there were only five of them all told. Nothing more was ever heard from Mungo Park, but it was ascertained that the survivors of the party being attacked by natives when their boat was run aground, jumped into the water and attempted to save themselves by swimming, but were all drowned. Thus died, at the age of thirty-one, one of the most intrepid of English adventurers. His manner in society was cold and reserved, but his face, by contrast, extraordinarily animated, and with the light of fanaticism in his eyes. The decision to start upon that last boat journey, with only five men of the original forty left—and one of them "deranged in his mind"—was surely one of the most heroic resolutions ever taken.

The mystery of the White Nile was solved (for all practical purposes) by perhaps the oddest figure, after Coryat's, in the whole portrait gallery of explorer adventurers. Richard Burton was a mixture of scholar, man of action, and eccentric Bohemian. He was believed to have gipsy blood in his veins, and boasted of an alleged left-handed connection between his family and the Bourbons, dating from the reign of the Grand Monarque. He was a born rebel and when, after being educated abroad and acquiring a surprising fluency in foreign tongues, he appeared at Oxford in 1840, with his wild eyes and a long dark moustache like a cavalry officer's, he was a sufficiently unusual kind of undergraduate to arouse comment. He challenged one of his critics to a duel and otherwise behaved in such a violent and unusual manner that he was eventually sent down without a degree, like many other good men before and after him. He next joined the Indian Army, but devoted all his time to the study of Oriental languages. In 1853, while still in the Army, he disguised himself as a Moslem pilgrim from Northern India and set out to explore the unknown interior of Arabia. He got no farther than Mecca and Medina, nor was he by any means the first European to visit these forbidden cities; but his journey had an exciting quality of its own (he was the sort of man who always has adventures anywhere), and his published account of it with its harsh, uncouth language, its extravagant opinions, and grim, ironic humour is one of the curiosities of travel literature.

This book made Burton famous, and the British Government formally commissioned him to search for the sources of the Nile. Accompanied by Lieutenant Speke he set out on a memorable journey which resulted in the discovery of the great lakes of Central Africa, from which the Nile is fed. They came upon the first of these, Lake Tanganyika, in February 1858; then Burton fell ill, and Speke, pushing on alone, found Victoria Nyanza. There was some jealousy between them which ended in a bitter quarrel. Burton, after further adventures in West Africa and elsewhere, entered the Consular Service, and occupied his leisure time with his famous translation of the *Arabian Nights*, a crude yet brilliant work which administered one of the severest shocks she ever received to the Victorian Mrs. Grundy. Burton has been described as an

Elizabethan born out of time; certainly his amazing intellectual versatility—quite apart from his jealous quarrelsome temper and his almost inhuman energy —seems to belong naturally to the sixteenth rather than the nineteenth century.

Speke and Grant continued Burton's work. In 1863, returning from Victoria Nyanza, they met that sturdy adventurer, Samuel Baker, moving with his train of porters in the direction from whence they had come. Baker was afraid that it would now be useless to proceed, since everything was already discovered. But Speke and Grant behaved like sportsmen; they gave him all the information they possessed, and sent him off on a quest which ended on the banks of the Albert Nyanza, the last of the three great lakes to be discovered.

If Burton was an Elizabethan adventurer born out of time, David Livingstone, a typical Victorian, seems to sum up in his own person all that was best in the gallant army of adventurers who added glory to the reign of the later Queen. Bible in hand (but too busy to do much expounding), raging against the iniquities of the slave trade, the corruption of Portuguese officials, his head buzzing with impossible ideals, yet his purpose so manifestly unselfish and pure, his manner so straightforward, and his simple, childish humour so infectious that he could do almost as he liked not only with native chiefs but also with Arabs and Europeans, he succeeded in penetrating to places even now regarded as inaccessible, so that his reports to the Royal Geographical Society were probably as rich in new information as any ever sent home by an explorer. A dour-looking, bony-faced man of swarthy complexion, oddly and untidily dressed, an unready speaker and using the English language so awkwardly (from lack of practice during his long residence among African natives, he used to say), Livingstone might easily have been mistaken for a foreigner, though in all the essentials he was, like many Scots, more English than the English.

It is impossible to follow him step by step through his many journeys; but the celebrated incident which occurred in 1871, in the course of his last expedition, cannot be omitted from any account of the Victorian adventurers. Livingstone, who had given up all connection with the missionary societies, and was now financed as an explorer by the Government, the Royal Geographical Society, and one or two wealthy men, started on this expedition in August 1865. His main objective was the study of the watershed between the Nyassa and Tanganyika lakes, after which "all questions about Central Africa will be definitely resolved"—and if we say "*major* questions" that characteristically cock-sure Victorian assertion is not so foolish after all. But in December 1866 one of Livingstone's native assistants arrived at Zanzibar with the tragic story of the death of the great traveller—how he had been attacked by Zulus, how almost unaided he had kept them at bay, shooting so coolly that a semi-circle of corpses lay before him, until one of the savages sprang in from behind and nearly severed his head from his body with a single fatal stroke.

There were certain discrepancies in this story which aroused suspicion; but it happened that at the same time all communications from Livingstone abruptly ceased, and after two or three years of complete silence Livingstone's admirers, both in England and America, became seriously alarmed. For nearly six years no one heard a word from him (he was desperately ill, as it turned out afterwards, and was far inland with no facilities for sending messages). But Edward Young led an expedition which proved that Livingstone had travelled, still in good health and spirits, far beyond the place where he was alleged to have been killed.

It was then that a rich American came to the rescue with one of those handsome gestures for which rich Americans are deservedly well known. Mr. Gordon Bennett, junior, son of the owner of the *New York Herald*, sent for a brilliant young war correspondent named H. M. Stanley, and privately instructed him to go and find Livingstone, and not to trouble about expense. "Take what you want, but find Livingstone," he said. Stanley, always a man of large ideas, took him at his word. Not the Manila ship itself, carrying the fabled wealth of the Golden West from Acapulco to Cadiz, held such a cargo of unexpected luxuries as did Stanley's argosy when he set out.

He showed himself at once to be an explorer of outstanding ability. After many wanderings, casting vaguely hither and thither but getting no definite news of his man, his caravan was one day approaching the native village of Ujiji, accompanied by the usual crowd of curious villagers who had come out to greet them, when Stanley was astounded to hear from among the sea of black faces a cordial "Good morning, sir!" pronounced in perfectly good English. It was Livingstone's servant. Almost speechless with excitement, his heart, as he tells us, beating fast, but determined not to act in a way that might "detract from the dignity of a white man," Stanley pushed his way through to the head of the crowd, which had reached the entrance to the village. There, waiting for him he saw a group of dignified Arab chiefs, in their flowing robes, and, standing a little in front of them, a white-haired, tired-looking European, with a half-incredulous smile upon his lips.

"I would have run to him, only I was a coward in the presence of such a mob—would have embraced him, but I did not know how he would receive me; so I did what moral cowardice and false pride suggested was the best thing—walked deliberately to him, took off my hat and said:

" '*Dr. Livingstone, I presume?*'

" 'Yes,' said he, with a kind, cordial smile, lifting his cap slightly.

"I replaced my hat on my head, and he replaced his cap, and we both grasped hands. I then said aloud:

" 'I thank God, doctor, I have been permitted to see you.'

"He answered: 'I feel thankful that I am here to welcome you.'"

If they had been Elizabethans they would have made more of that scene. As it is we feel that the American-trained Stanley, with only a little encouragement, might have risen to the occasion. They went into the house together. There were copies of the *Saturday Review* and *Punch* lying about on the floor. They talked; but Stanley was so excited that he could never afterwards remember what they said. One thing, however, he did remember, when it was almost too late. As Livingstone talked he observed his wasted features, his teeth all broken and worn "from the hard fare of Lunda" and heard him say that his stomach refused everything except an occasional cup of tea.

"'Oh, by George!' I said, 'I have forgotten something. Hasten, Selim, and bring that bottle: you know which: and bring me the silver goblets. I brought this bottle on purpose for this event, which I hoped would come to pass, though often it seemed useless to expect it.'

"Selim knew where the bottle was, and he soon returned with it—a bottle of Sillery champagne; and, handing the Doctor a silver goblet brimful of the exhilarating wine, and pouring a small quantity into my own, I said:

"'Dr. Livingstone, to your very good health, sir.'

"'And to yours,' he responded smilingly."

That little scene shows the whiskered century at its best. Apparently they finished the bottle together. But Stanley goes on, rather unnecessarily, to insist that Livingstone was at all ordinary times a severely temperate man; and also that he never forgot to shave his chin (though not his cheeks) every morning. He was now, by Mr. Gordon Bennett's generosity, supplied with good and plentiful food for the first time for years, and he spent many happy hours in Stanley's company. Stanley left in March 1872; and a year later Livingstone died in a village on the banks of Molilamo, and his body was brought back to England and buried in Westminster Abbey.

Stanley, as may be seen from the above quotations, had a pleasant trick of lively narrative, which Livingstone never possessed. We have called him American-trained, but he was born in Wales, and it was only the accident of the presence in London of Mr. Gordon Bennett, when young Stanley, as a war correspondent, sent home the first news of the end of the Abyssinian campaign, that took him across the Atlantic. His easy, fluent style, and the rapidity and decision with which he would "go after" his "story" and send it home in front of all his rivals endeared him to the heart of his new employer, the founder of a school of journalism which was then regarded as alarmingly sensational. By the time he returned from his visit to Livingstone, it was recognised that he possessed not only exceptional grit and powers of organisation, but also that rare authority and influence with savages which is the explorer's greatest gift. With his European assistants he usually quarrelled, for he was a hard disciplinarian, arbitrary in manner, who seldom forgave a fault, or forgot to mention it in his public narrative. But natives seem invariably to have adored him.

His greatest feat, of course, was the founding of

the Congo Free State, and when one comes to think of it hardly any Englishman in the whole history of adventurous exploration has a more substantial achievement to his credit. To equal it we have to go back to the days of the Spanish conquistadores. Other explorers have found new countries, but they have usually left to later hands the turning of them into organised states. Starting from the farthest point reached by Livingstone, Stanley sailed down the Congo till he reached the Atlantic Ocean, having penetrated the very heart of Africa. He at once saw the commercial value of this great waterway, and returning to England he spent over a year trying to persuade the British public and British capitalists to support him in taking it over and putting the whole district under the Union Jack. The King of the Belgians, who had been interested in the project from the start, waited tactfully; until Stanley in despair crossed over to Brussels and offered to lead a Belgian expedition instead. The rest of the story is well known. It may be added, however, that when it was too late, not only England, but Germany and other European Powers waked up to the fact that King Leopold had stolen a march on them. Whereupon the general scramble for Africa began.

But Stanley's adventures were not finished. He frequently visited East Africa, and ended up with the exploit which perhaps won him more popular fame than any other—his great march to the relief of Emin Pasha, who, as it turned out, neither needed nor desired to be relieved. The Pasha, a German by birth, in the service of the Egyptian Government, had been driven south by the rebellion of the Mahdi and had carved out for himself a very comfortable little principality in Wadelai. However, Stanley, with his masterful way, was always difficult to resist, and Emin allowed himself to be "saved" and to return with his rescuers to Zanzibar.

CHAPTER X

THE SIEGE OF THE POLES

THE Napoleonic Wars, like the Civil War of the seventeenth century, inevitably acted as a brake upon English exploration, because all the born explorers and adventurers were busy fighting. In one sense, of course, war is the adventurer's opportunity; it gives an opening to many a brave-spirited lad who might otherwise have found himself fettered to an office stool. But in the case of the genius, the great man of action, who could never, in any case, have been held down, it too often does nothing but harm, by giving him an official number and placing him in the ranks, one among a number of fighting-machines. War does not always encourage initiative, and the young officer who—as Nelson did—makes a practice of assuming dangerous and unnecessary responsibilities, is just as often frowned on as praised.

From the English point of view, the conflict with Napoleon was, in the main, a naval conflict. For a matter of nearly twenty years, with one short interval, our fleets were at sea, fully manned, and their time well occupied in watching the French ports, dealing with any enemy fleet that put out, and acting against American rebels, hostile privateers and other destroyers of commerce. There was small opportunity for naval officers to engage in private adventures or lead scientific expeditions to the remoter parts of the globe.

Yet any reader who has followed me so far will have recognised the increasing share that naval officers are taking in English exploration. Most of the great navigators in the eighteenth century had been trained in the Navy. And now with the dawn of the nineteenth there opened out the wide and alluring prospect of a new kind of adventure, as dramatic and inspiring as any ever thought of, and one of which the naval officer was the obvious, ideal leader—the siege of the two Poles. He must have been a youth of sluggish imagination who did not long to take part in some of those voyages to the frozen North, when new headlands, new bays and rivers and mountains, were added to the map by each succeeding expedition. Nelson himself, as a boy of fifteen, had visited the Arctic in the *Racehorse* and fought his famous duel with the polar bear. Nelson had the independent spirit of the true adventurer if ever any man had it; but it is significant that he never found time to fight polar bears again. England needed him.

But with the close of the Napoleonic Wars and the removal of the menace which had so long kept every European nation standing on guard, all this bottled-up enthusiasm for adventure and this curiosity about the grey unknown North was everywhere let loose. We have noted that Bligh of the *Bounty*—and of the great *Bounty* boat voyage—was present at the Battle of Copenhagen and was sent for by Nelson and personally thanked by the little hero for his services. By a coincidence, we begin at the same place, and on the same occasion, in taking note of the first of the great Arctic explorers, John Franklin.

Franklin, like Nelson, was an East Anglian. Having early declared his determination to go to sea, his father, who was opposed to the project, very foolishly sent him to rough it on a merchantman, thinking that the hardships would cure his passion. They only increased it; and at Copenhagen, in 1801, young Franklin found himself serving as a midshipman on the *Polyphemus* (74), which was at the northern end of Nelson's line, and therefore came in for a hammering, not only from the opposing ships in the Danish line, but also from the powerful land battery (the Crown) on the starboard side. This was Franklin's baptism of fire. Four years later he was at Trafalgar, winning distinction as signalling officer on the *Bellerophon*. In the interval, however, he had served under Flinders for three years, mapping the coast of Australia (a reminder that exploration did not entirely cease at this time[1]) and gradually winning recognition as the type of officer, half scientist, half adventurer, who was at his best in the work of exploration. At the same time his square, bulldog jaw and sturdy figure, his pleasant manner and imperturbable calm in moments of danger marked him out as a leader of men.

[1] But it should be noted that the gallant Flinders was arrested by the French on his way home, and imprisoned for six and a half years on the island of Mauritius, to the ruination of his health, so that he died, a broken-hearted man, on the very day that his book recording the labour of his life was published (July 1814).

Young Franklin returned home from Australia on a merchant ship, forming part of a fleet of eleven East Indiamen, under Commodore Nathaniel Dance, of John Company, sailing together without any escort. In the Straits of Malacca they were sighted by a French squadron, consisting of five men-of-war, a line-of-battle ship, two large frigates, a corvette and a brig, who made sail joyfully to intercept them, for East Indiamen were always rich prizes. There followed an incident unique in the annals of the sea. Instead of surrendering, Nathaniel Dance (who was perhaps encouraged by the presence on board of a number of naval officers and men from Flinders's expedition) got his great, lumbering merchantmen into a straggling line of battle and prepared to fight. In those days an East Indiaman carried from thirty to thirty-six guns, so that if their crews really showed fight and their gunnery was anything like accurate they might, by sheer weight of metal, keep the Frenchmen off, though the feat would be unexampled.

As a matter of fact Linois, the French admiral, observing their bold front, came to the conclusion that they must be men-of-war in disguise. He approached warily, with the idea of cutting off the rearmost ships. What was his astonishment when, at Dance's signal, the whole line of merchantmen tacked "in succession" in the orthodox naval manner, and bore down upon him to engage. Franklin was acting as signal officer on Dance's East Indiaman, and had the pleasure of hoisting this remarkable signal. The action which followed had lasted only three-quarters of an hour, when the

French made sail to get away. Franklin, at Dance's orders, immediately ran up the signal for a general chase, amid roars of cheers from the other English ships. Then was seen the shocking spectacle of a distinguished French admiral and his squadron of five making all sail to get away from a pursuing crowd of armed merchantmen. Dance chased for two hours, just to say he had done it, and then continued on his homeward course.

Franklin got his first important command in 1818, when he sailed in command of the *Trent*, in company with Captain Buchan in the *Dorothea*, with orders from the Admiralty to find the North Pole! They got no farther than Spitzbergen, and the general results of the expedition were purely negative. But Franklin, as a commander, had made such a good impression that in the following year he was sent in charge of an important land expedition to explore the central part of the northern shore of Arctic America, with a view to solving the ancient riddle of the North-west Passage. Two sea expeditions were to co-operate. It is extraordinary that the Government should still have been pursuing this unpractical will-o'-the-wisp. In 1818, when Franklin was at Spitzbergen, an Act of Parliament was solemnly passed authorising a reward of £20,000 to the first man who should "find a northern passage between the Atlantic and Pacific Oceans." No one ever claimed the reward, and ten years later the offer was withdrawn. But it may be as well to state here that in 1850 a certain Captain McClure did actually reach the Behring Straits from the Pacific, though to do so he had to abandon his

ship and walk some hundreds of miles over ice.
Finally Amundsen brought a vessel right through
in 1906—a gallant feat which it seems extremely
unlikely that any sane person will ever attempt to
imitate.

Franklin's land expedition did much good work,
and also suffered appalling hardships. They win-
tered at Fort Enterprise on the banks of Winter
Lake; but before the cold weather had fully set in
they were already short of provisions. A young
officer named Back accordingly set out on snow-
shoes for the nearest station of the Hudson Bay
Company, a distance of 1100 miles, with nothing
to cover him at nights except a deerskin and a single
blanket, and brought back fresh supplies. Franklin
failed to get in touch with the ships of the sea
expeditions, and therefore started to return over
land.

It was a terrible journey. The starving men
subsisted mainly on *tripe de roche*, a kind of lichen
with a bitter, unsatisfying taste. If they shot an
animal they devoured it raw. They had made
arrangements with friendly Indians for food supplies
to be placed at certain points *en route*; but the
Indians had failed them; there was no food, and
they were driven to eating shoe-leather. One of the
half-castes with the party, a man named Michel,
murdered two of his companions and feasted on
their bodies. He was shot by an Englishman. Then
a herd of reindeer appeared quite close to them; but
by this time the wretched men were too weak to
raise a gun to shoot at them. One by one they died,
the British seamen, curiously enough, bearing up

much better than the native Canadians. When they were at the last gasp three friendly Indians arrived with provisions, having been sent to the rescue by the indefatigable Mr. Back, who had gone on ahead.

In 1825 Franklin led another and much more ambitious expedition to the same regions. His reward was a knighthood. In 1829, he was in command of H.M.S. *Rainbow* off the Greek coast during the War of Independence; and from 1836 to 1843 he occupied, with dignity and success, the difficult post of Lieutenant-Governor of Tasmania (then called Van Diemen's Land). He returned to England in 1844 at an age when most men would have been content to retire. But hearing that yet another Arctic expedition was being fitted out, for the pursuit of the elusive Passage, he at once applied for the command. He was coldly informed that the Admiralty could not think of appointing a man of sixty. "You have been misinformed, my Lord," replied Franklin indignantly, "I am only fifty-nine." They gave him the command, and he set sail with two ships, the *Erebus* and the *Terror*, provisioned for three years, and manned by picked volunteers from the Navy.

In Baffin's Bay he was sighted by some whalers. And after that there was complete silence, extending from weeks into months, and from months into years. At first there was no serious alarm; but in June 1848, after three years of silence, a relief ship was sent out. It found nothing. Another was dispatched, then another, and another. The searchers for Franklin made great geographical discoveries, and were properly rewarded for them. But no one ever found Franklin alive; and it was not until 1857 that McClintock, by the discovery of some hurriedly written messages enclosed in bottles, was enabled to trace the tragic story of the ruin of Franklin's last expedition—the loss of both his ships, and the death from exhaustion and privation of their crews.

The siege of the North Pole continued without intermission. The names of such men as Parry, Markham, and Nares spring to the mind. But gradually the initiative was allowed to slip out of English hands. Norwegians and Americans, as a glance at the map will show, had a territorial advantage: they started each race for the Pole some hundreds of miles in front of us. It would be beyond the scope of this book to describe the exploits of Nansen and Peary and other foreign explorers; but it may be briefly noted that Peary, who was the inventor of the system of living on the dogs—that is, working them to death and eating them when they fell—made a final dash northward in 1909, and reached a point which, if it was not actually the Pole (for the late Sir Clements Markham has pointed out what very rough calculations Peary made to fix his position) was at any rate near enough.

To scientific geographers, of course, this race to the Pole seemed a futile waste of time; Sir Clements Markham expressed their point of view when, after Peary's success, he uttered the earnest hope that "there will now be an end of the North Pole," except as a point on the map, and that in future explorers would turn to more useful work. The average reader will not readily admit that. He will feel instinctively that the great adventure, after all, was to set foot on the axis of the earth. And he will sympathise with the man who would sacrifice anything, and let scientific observation go hang, in order to do so. Within the last few years the North Pole has been flown over and seen from the air; and it is from the air, no doubt, that its privacy will be finally destroyed and the curiosity of the scientists satisfied. In the meantime, the ordinary man will take off his hat to Peary.

The story of the South Pole siege is curiously different. There is, indeed, remarkably little in common between the two Polar regions—the North with its towering icebergs, its polar bears, its Esquimaux and reindeer not so far away; and the South with its smooth flat bergs, just showing their surfaces like so many floating tables, its absence of human and most other kinds of life, its long uninterrupted silence, year in and year out, broken only by the soft padding of the penguins' feet or the hoarse bark of a seal. The South, during all the latter part of the nineteenth century and the beginning of this was the special province of the English explorers, who found convenient jumping-off places in New Zealand and the Falkland Islands.

Sir James Ross started south in 1839. He had been engaged in the work of exploration since the age of eighteen, and now, at thirty-nine, he was one of the most experienced and efficient explorers who ever left these shores. His immediate purpose was to reach the magnetic pole; but after passing through the pack he found his further progress in

that direction arrested by the presence of land, and
therefore turned southwards, until he discovered an
unknown sea (now called the Ross Sea), and sailing
through that found himself opposite the Great Ice
Barrier, always a wonderful sight, but the more
wonderful to these early explorers by whom it was
totally unexpected. Ross wrote:

As we approached the land under all studding-
sails we perceived a low white line extending
from its eastern extreme point as far as the eye
could discern to the eastward. It presented an
extraordinary appearance, gradually increasing in
height as we got nearer to it, and proving at
length to be a perpendicular cliff of ice, between
one hundred and fifty and two hundred feet above
the level of the sea, perfectly flat and level at the
top, and without any fissures or promontories on
its even seaward face.

He coasted along the barrier for two hundred and
fifty miles, making careful observations, and when
he returned to England in 1843 had done much to
strengthen the belief of those who had always held
that a large southern continent must surround the
Pole. At the same time, it was not, and still is not
proved that the various blocks of land discovered
are all connected together.

There followed a long and inexplicable pause—
an interval of no less than sixty years—before
another serious attempt was made to storm the
defences of the South Pole. By the discovery of the
Ross Sea an important and obvious breach had been

made in them. It only waited to be exploited. Why so long a period should have elapsed before the next expedition appeared remains a mystery. But with the advent of Scott and Shackleton, we are in our own times. Their deaths are so recent and the main outline of their gallant careers so well remembered that it would be waste of time to go over them again here.

Scott was of a type unusual among explorers— almost as unexpected as Dampier, though in a different way. If he had not been sent into the Navy as a child he might easily have adopted some sedentary way of life. Sir James Barrie has told us how, on the occasion of his first meeting with the explorer, they tramped the streets of London half the night—each allowing the other to escort him home and then insisting on returning the compliment—arguing out an ancient quarrel, "the comparison," to quote Sir James, "of the life of action (which he pooh-poohed) with the loathly life of those who sit at home (which I scorned)." It is common enough to find a literary man longing for a life of action; it is much less common to find a man of action envying those who sit at home.

Scott's nickname as a boy was "Old Mooney," and, though everybody liked him, his absent-mindedness and laziness almost drove his friends to despair. He hated any kind of brutality. It is impossible to doubt that his objection to the use of dogs in polar exploration was largely based on sentiment, though he could give many other reasons for it. All his life he suffered nausea at the sight of blood; to accustom himself to it he would deli-

berately sit and watch the zoologists of the *Discovery*
skinning dead animals. But if this softer side of
his nature was, in some respects, a weakness, it was
also his strength. Few leaders have been loved and
trusted as Scott was. Few men of action could have
written those gentle, almost intolerably moving
words in that lonely tent amidst the Antarctic snows
before the pencil fell from his fingers, and he (the
last to go because always the last to lose heart) lay
back to die between his two dead companions,
throwing out his arm with a last gesture across the
body of Wilson, his life-long friend.

In the long and glorious history of exploration,
insufficient attention has been given—or so it seems
to a mere outsider—to the luck of the weather.
Some men, as every stay-at-home knows, are lucky
with the weather; some are not. Scott comes under
the second category. I have no intention of re-
telling the famous story of his last expedition in
detail. It was the best equipped that had ever left
this or any other country. It would be the greatest
mistake in the world to think of it as a mere dash
for the Pole. That was to be its culminating effort;
but, in the meantime, a numerous staff of scientific
experts had accumulated a large collection of specimens, had surveyed and re-mapped the country for
many miles, and had prepared photographs and
cinema films, which, when they were shown in
London, at once disclosed to the general public
that the survivors of Scott's expedition had come
home with more new information about the
Antarctic than any other explorers before their time
or since. At one stroke the general appearance and

character of the Great White South, of which no one but a few experts had hitherto pretended to know anything, was brought home forcibly and visibly to the ordinary man in the street. If Scott had never attempted that fatal polar journey his position in the ranks of the great explorers was already assured.

But of course he must try for it. He would never have been an explorer at all if he had not felt that. He strove to keep his sense of proportion. When he heard that Amundsen was at the Bay of Whales on the other side of the Ross Sea preparing to make a rush for the Pole with his dogs, Scott refused to change his plans or put forward his dates, but went on steadily until the main work of the expedition was almost completed, and his polar party could start, according to plan. On 18th January 1912, accompanied by Captain Oates, Lieutenant Bowers, Dr. Wilson, and Petty-Officer Evans, he arrived at the South Pole. And there, in the snow and bitter cold of "this awful place," as Scott calls it, they found a small tent and a Norwegian flag, telling them that they were forestalled. Amundsen had been there a month before. I can never get it out of my mind that this cruel disappointment must have weakened their wills on the return journey—though, of course, they would have never admitted it, and perhaps did not know it themselves. On the first day of the long drag back, Scott wrote in his private diary: "Well, we have turned our back now on the goal of our ambition, and must face our eight hundred miles of solid dragging—and good-bye to most of the daydreams!" The thought of a "daydream" fulfilled and the welcome awaiting them in England would have stayed them up better than the most plentiful rations.

The rest of the story of this great Antarctic tragedy is quickly told. Evans weakened and died, and was left at the foot of the Beardmore Glacier; but precious time was lost in trying to get him along. The weather was always against them. Oates's feet were frostbitten, and, though he urged them to leave him, they would not, and this caused further delays. The relief party which was waiting for them at a pre-arranged point used up all its rations and was compelled to return to the base. Then a blizzard came on, blowing in their faces and exhausting their last reserves of strength. Early one morning Oates got out of his sleeping-bag and said that he was going outside the tent, and "I may be some time." What he did was to walk blindly into the blizzard, caring neither for time nor direction, seeking only that lonely death which he hoped might save the lives of his companions by relieving them of his weight on the sledges. There was something about this act of self-sacrifice which appealed powerfully to the imagination of the nation when the full story was told. Alas, it came too late! A day or two more, the blizzard still raging, and Scott, Bowers, and Wilson had reached the limit of their endurance. When they died they were only eleven miles from the first food depot.

In the same year (1909) that Peary found the North Pole, a party detached from one of Ernest Shackleton's expeditions arrived on the site of Ross's old objective, the magnetic South. Shackleton himself was busy delivering the most dangerous attack that had yet been made upon the inner defences of the *geographical* South Pole. He made his way up the side of the formidable Beardmore Glacier, which is more than twice the size of any other glacier known, and, reaching the top, plunged boldly southward into the unknown. He was about a hundred miles from the Pole when his food supplies ran out and he had to turn back. Shackleton had served with Scott, but was of a very different type. He could never have been anything but a man of action. He was big, quiet, simple, and deeply religious. One of the memories of him which can never die is his description of how, when he and another were crossing the snow-swept island of South Georgia, to bring help to the exhausted comrades whom they had been compelled to leave behind, they caught themselves again and again imagining that there was someone else with them, a third traveller. Shackleton, in his book, does not hesitate to advance a purely religious explanation of this phenomenon, and further concludes that it was only by divine assistance that he was able to surmount all the dangers and difficulties of this journey and rescue his friends.

Another picture that sticks in the memory is that of Shackleton's tall figure striding gloomily up and down the single street of the little town of Stanley in the Falkland Islands, waiting for news of the ships with which he hoped to go to the help of Wild and his men left behind on Whale Island. Day after day he waited. Soon it would be too late. The mental strain might have been too much for a man of more elaborate psychology. But Shackleton kept his nerve, and, in due course, arrived with the rescue party at Whale Island and had the joy of seeing his men still alive and well. He died on board ship on the way out to his last expedition. He died in harness, as Scott did.

CHAPTER XI

OUR OWN TIMES

WE may now bid a final farewell to the frozen icefields, the twilight skies and everlasting snows of the polar regions, and turn for a moment eastward, refreshing our spirits with the fragrant breezes of the Spice Islands and warming our hands at the golden glow of the eastern sun. Because, after all, the adventurers of the nineteenth century were not invariably explorers; and it is right to mention at least one name among those who during all this period continued to advance their own fortunes—and often those of their country at the same time—in that ancient oriental theatre of human endeavour.

We have seen something of conditions in India at the close of the eighteenth century, and of the rare prospects of lucrative adventure which they offered to soldiers of fortune; and we have seen how those opportunities were taken, and that English military adventurers—in spite of the difficulty of regularising their position *vis-à-vis* the Home Government—were seldom behindhand in the race. But as English influence gradually spread over the whole of India, European military adventurers of the type of Perron or Thomas or Skinner (who had at least fourteen wives) found no scope for their activities, and either went elsewhere or entered the service of the East India Company. In that service they would get plenty of opportunities of promotion and adventure—but adventure now definitely of the official sort, and therefore excluded from our survey. The Company's servants in all but name were officials of the British Government, and the military officers in their pay cannot, obviously, be classified as adventurers merely because they held no commissions from the Crown.

That was the position in India. But elsewhere in the East the field was still open. It must be remembered that Stamford Raffles only arrived at the new trading settlement of Penang in 1805. It was not until 1819 that he induced the British Government to annex Singapore—which Hamilton had refused as a gift a century earlier. In many parts of the Malay Peninsula and about the islands the inhabitants had never seen or heard of a white man; the local pirates who had made themselves a nuisance in the days of Hamilton were still going strong; independent sultans waged war upon each other without fear of interference by the British or any other European Government. Here was the true adventurer's opportunity.

Whole books might be written—and have been for all I know—about the exploits of English adventurers in the East Indies in the first half of the nineteenth century. But one name springs immediately to the mind—that of Rajah Brooke of Sarawak. I shall take Rajah Brooke as typical. Sarawak, which now borders Borneo on its western side, formed in 1839 the southernmost province of the Sultanate of Brunei. It was in rebellion against the Sultan when James Brooke first appeared on the scene and gave valuable help in suppressing the insurrection. The Sultan was so grateful that he made the Englishman governor of Sarawak, and Brooke, in company with Captain Keppel, proceeded to expel the pirates from the rivers and generally clean things up. In 1850 the Chinese, who formed a large proportion of the population, rose in rebellion with the intention of massacring the English and seizing the country for themselves. They were promptly and forcibly put down. There has been no serious trouble in Sarawak since. The power of Brunei decayed; but Sarawak under its English governor prospered, until in 1863 the British Government, after much hesitation, recognised its independence, and the place is ruled by descendants of Rajah Brooke to this day.

That date—1863—turns our thoughts westward, for it was the decisive date of the American Civil War. Both from the point of view of the numbers engaged and its strategical and tactical significance it is a war that has received less attention than it deserves from English critics. But in those days it was our custom to sneer at all things, good or bad, that came from America, just as nowadays we loudly praise them. For the moment, our point is that Englishmen fought on both sides in that war; though more for the South than for the North, because there was something about the Southern cause which appealed to the individualism which is an essential part of every adventurer's character. There were other nineteenth-century wars which offered similar opportunities. Byron and Trelawney in Greece had given their all in the cause of a little nation, struggling to be free. If I do not pause to recount their exploits it is because I know very well —and every honest reader of this book knows in his heart—that there is a kind of adventure that is really an artist's adventure, an adventure of the soul rather than of the body, a purely intellectual gesture which may or may not entail some physical action, by way of emphasis. When Byron went to Greece he was paying a debt to his conscience, excusing himself to Heaven, and doing the thing thoroughly like the brave man he was. But it is absurd to call these sensation-hunters adventurers. You would not call a rich tourist in a motor car a traveller, though he can sometimes get to places that honest travellers seldom reach.

The Spanish Legion was quite a different affair. Its leader, De Lacy Evans, was a regular soldier who had served under Wellington in the Peninsula and at Quatre Bras and Waterloo. He was a Liberal Member of Parliament when, in 1835, he was sent out to Spain to help Queen Isabella against the Legitimist Pretender, Don Carlos. Although the expedition had official backing, his officers were mainly volunteers, and the whole affair had the authentic note of adventure. Evans, who showed himself a capable commander, won several victories against heavy odds and was afterwards given an important command in the Crimean War.

No doubt there were also Englishmen in the later wars of the century. Lord Kitchener himself served as a volunteer on the French side in the War of 1870. There were Englishmen helping the Greeks against the Turks and the Turks against the Greeks in 1897; there were Englishmen and Germans assisting the Moorish rebels only a few years ago; and, until the popular press and the cinema began to make a sentimental "stunt" of it there were always Englishmen in the French Foreign Legion. There was an Englishman, named Beard, I think, who served under that adventurous blackguard, Enver Pasha, in 1912, when the Arabs of Tripoli were organised to resist the Italian occupation. It was a hopeless adventure. The Englishman was killed, and Enver himself, on the outbreak of the Balkan Wars, was smuggled back to Turkey, with the unofficial connivance of British officials in Egypt, to bring his country into the Great War against us and cause the death by starvation and torture of the greater part of the British garrison of Kut el-Amara.

There were Englishmen in those days who knew the coasts of Arabia and the forbidden cities of the East better than it was convenient to say. C. M. Doughty's incomparable book, *Arabia Deserta*, was the result of a series of journeys which were unique, like the book itself. There is somewhere in the English character an affinity with the Bedouin— with the man who travels day after day upon that beautifully sensitive piece of mechanism called "the ship of the desert," his eyes always straining, as a sailor's do, towards some distant oasis or landfall. We know his strength and his weakness, his passionate loyalties and his childish, brooding superstitions. Puritanism flourishes in the desert, as it does at sea. At this moment, under the rule of the Wahabis, it is a criminal offence to smoke a cigarette anywhere in Arabia, and a public outrage to drink a glass of beer. And this strange state of affairs, linking Mecca and New York in a kind of unnatural alliance, is likely to continue until the Egyptians come to their senses and, remembering the great days of Mohammed Ali and Ibrahim, take their puritanical neighbour by the scruff of the neck and insist upon his conforming to civilised usage. For strange though it may sound to modern ears the Egyptians were once men enough, under the Albanian leader, Ibrahim, to conquer the warlike Wahabis and drive them out of the holy land of Islam, which they now occupy again. And it was in that little-known desert campaign in the second decade of the century that the gallant Scottish adventurer, Keith, sacrificed his life to save the Egyptian Prince Toussoun. Serving in the ranks of the 78th Regiment, Keith had been taken prisoner at the disastrous battle of Rosetta, when Fraser's expedition went to ruin, and had with many others been led into Cairo through jeering mobs insulting them and making mock of their Scottish uniforms, and marched through the Ezbekieh Gardens between avenues of poles bearing the severed heads of British soldiers. Somehow he had attracted notice and become a Moslem, and had risen to be the young pasha's most trusted lieutenant.

And mention of Arabia recalls "Lawrence of Arabia." We are now arrived at the Great War, and in every sideshow, all over the world, there are adventurers by the dozen each one of them deserving his paragraph in this book. At sea the Germans had all the best of it. English naval adventurers—the survivors of Scott's expedition, for instance—were absorbed into the fleet; but on the German side only individual adventurers got a chance to assert themselves—and men like Luckner and Muller did not miss it. On land, however, the wide dispersion of the English effort, holding everywhere, as we did, the outer lines, gave our modern youth an opportunity of proving that we were still the most adventurous nation in the world.

T. E. Lawrence was an Oxford don when he volunteered for active service and went to Cairo to translate Arabic documents for the British G.H.Q. That he should have so quickly impressed his personality upon that august but insensitive body was not the least of his achievements. Every schoolboy knows—not as Macaulay used the phrase, but in literal fact—every schoolboy knows how he was sent over to Arabia, adopted Arab dress, assisted King Feisal to organise the Arab army, developed a genius for guerrilla warfare, and rode into Damascus with the Arab irregulars in 1918. These things could not escape attention, and anyhow, his own account of the matter immediately became a best-seller (and will rank for ever as a classic of travel literature). Moreover the very theatricality of his attempts to dodge the limelight ensured that he could never keep out of it. He became the hero of the popular press and of the writers of popular biographies, and the leading villain in enemy propaganda. As I write these words, his alleged activities in some underground office in Whitehall (in reality he is serving as a private soldier in India) are being made the excuse

by the Soviet authorities in Russia for the staging
of an elaborate "conspiracy plot," with a view to
arousing patriotic indignation in the proletariat.

Again we are confronted with the fact that
Lawrence, this magnificent little adventurer, has
neither the physique, nor the temperament, nor the
training usually associated with the adventurer's
career. There is not even anything specially English
about him. But he has pre-eminently that dazzling,
eccentric genius which always makes the most
interesting adventurers, if not the most successful.
But for the War, such men as Lawrence might never
have taken to the life of adventure. That is the
importance of the War, from the point of view of
this short history. It cramped the style of some
adventurers; to others it brought an incentive and
an opportunity. Others again, who were adventurers before the War, and could never have been
anything else, found in it their last great adventure,
and too often paid for it with their lives. F. C.
Selous, the African hunter, was one of these. He
was killed in a comparatively unimportant skirmish
in East Africa, after rendering valuable services to
the British troops as a guide. It seemed a pity; but
as Selous would have been the first to admit, the
War had to come before all private adventures.
The War was *England's* adventure.[1]

We approach the last and infinitely the most
difficult stage of our journey—our own times. It is
a period of hero-worship and adventure-worship.
It would be absurd to deny that it is an adventurous

[1] Even now I find that I have forgotten Kaid Maclean of
Morocco! But it is too late for an apology.

age, writing, as I am, within a few weeks of the death of a Minister of the Crown in an experimental flight in an airship which crashed in France. But the difficulty is just that—that we talk so much about "romance" and "adventure" in our particular cheap-jack modern way, that the thing itself, which is there all the time never fear, is lost sight of in a sea of sentimental newspaper slops. The more we shout about our adventurers, the obscurer they become. All one can ever see of them is an occasional glimpse over the heads of a cheering mob of boy scouts and girl guides. Though they talk on the wireless every night we never hear their voices. Though they give daily and lengthy interviews to "special correspondents," we never know their minds. A mere clamour of meaningless noise, a mask of exasperating artificiality obscures their every word and deed, until one wishes that a man like Colonel Lindbergh had been born before the invention of the printing press so that we might get to know something about him.

Such is the din and the dust that it becomes almost impossible to distinguish one figure from another. You know that there are as many English adventurers here as in any period of our history; but you feel inclined to throw up your hands in despair and declare that the task of sorting them out is one for posterity when our inferior ink shall have become illegible, and our cheap paper fallen into rags, and only the soberer records will remain. It may, however, be suggested tentatively that there is a secure niche in the Temple of Fame for the two Englishmen, Alcock and Brown, who were the first to fly the Atlantic. They received curiously little notice. We hear much more of the first man to fly it alone, the first to fly it backwards (that is from west to east), the first woman to get across, and so forth. But the unostentatious achievement of Alcock and Brown will surely be given its proper place some day.

The craze for record-breaking, a fine thing in itself, has become a mere stupidity. The first woman to visit Timbuctoo (why should any woman visit Timbuctoo?); the first party to travel from the Cape to Cairo by motor car (one of the slowest and most inconvenient methods imaginable); the first to bicycle over some place eminently unsuitable for cycling; the first to drive a car at a speed at which no sane human being would ever wish to travel— exploits like these almost make one forget the extraordinary courage and endurance of those who perform them. We have to keep reminding ourselves that, after all, the journey is the thing, and that the goal doesn't really matter, even if it be more futile and infinitely less romantic than El Dorado.

It seems difficult to deny that the gallant and persistent attempts to climb Mount Everest come under the same category, though, for some indefinable reason, one respects them more. Yet "indefinable" is not the word. It is a question of prolonged human effort with a deadly risk at the end of it, as opposed to the risk alone. The summit of Mount Everest must surely be explored for the first time from the air. The air is the route by which we shall in future visit and observe all inaccessible places. But the first man who sees the summit of the world's highest mountain from an aeroplane will merely have broken another record; whereas Mallory and Irvine, who died in the attempt, did something more—they achieved an adventure.

The sky, with its aerial uncharted ways, is the new and characteristic field of modern adventure. Though, from the point of view of the adventurous traveller, it may curtail the journey and cut out much of the romance, it is our great hope for the future. Your true adventurer has never shown any sentimental hankering for out-of-date methods of transport; he likes to move briskly. The ships of the buccaneers were swift on the wing; Hawkwood's men were great marchers; and no one could teach Cœur de Lion anything new in the most expeditious means of reducing a fortress. It is true, of course, as Mr. de la Mare has recently pointed out in this connection, that it is distance that lends enchantment to the view, and that if we continue to contract our world by flying there may soon be "no wild and far for which to pine." Yet a man need not travel far to realise how absurdly small a portion of the earth's surface has, in that rather objectionable modern phrase, been "opened up." Probably most of the people in the world have never seen an Englishman, and most of the earth's surface has never felt the pressure of an English foot. Neither is a penny the worse for it. Nor is the Englishman. On the contrary he should rejoice that so much remains to be seen. And I think he may safely take wings unto himself, and look down at it from the air (if that will satisfy him) as the easiest and most expeditious method, without any fear that

it will become too familiar to be interesting either
in his own lifetime or that of his children or his
children's children.

The policeman—that enemy of adventure, who is
always trying to choke it (yet often feeds it with his
own life blood like a mother pelican)—can never be
more than a local phenomenon. The idea of a world
thoroughly policed all over is a dream, and—as Von
Moltke said in another connection—not even a
beautiful dream. It is a nightmare, born of in-
digestion brought on by too much pap. No single
human notion has ever been enforced upon the
whole world and, one hopes, never will be. For
variety is the very spice and essence of adventure.
It keeps us on the alert: it keeps us armed. And
while men's ideas of what is seemly and what is not,
what is fun and what is not, of religion and of civilisation, differ so widely, it is hard to see how we can
ever attain that unanimity, that complete, universal
placidity which is the reformer's ideal and the
adventurer's despair. Even when black men and
yellow men and brown men have been so carefully
educated and "civilised" as to be intellectually
indistinguishable from the white ones; and when we
have all got together round a table and agreed to
stop quarrelling and fighting, and have taken the
very last of our beautiful swords and beaten it into
a ploughshare; even then the wise man (if there be
one left) will not lose hope, but will wait with interest
to see the first angry idealist shy a stone.

No, the naval and military adventurers need not
fear. Nor need the explorers. When every farthest
sea has been charted and every square mile of land

surveyed, there will always be the amusing adventure of discovering how much they have missed. And even the hunter, that great adventurer, will not find his occupation gone, though the whole world turn vegetarian. When the Chocktaws and the Eskimaux (who, poor devils, will find it hard enough to obtain the necessary supplies of greenstuffs) and the flat-faced pygmies of the African swamps have all come to a cordial agreement with the London and New York vegetarian societies that it is wrong to kill an animal for food and fiendish to slay it for sport, even then there will remain that most exciting and delicate of adventurous careers—in which I imagine every out-of-work hunter will at once enrol himself—that of preventing the lions and tigers from being unkind to the harmless deer. The life of a (presumably) unarmed keeper in a vast and ever-growing game reserve will certainly not be lacking in incident.

But this is mere guessing. The point to make is that the life adventurous will not cease, however depressed and miserable this dim, grey, post-War world may become. It is rather stimulated by the lack of inducement to remain moping at home. Every dangerous polar expedition, every experimental voyage in an airship produces more applications for admission than the organisers are able to deal with. Every South American rebel army that takes the field could add to its ranks a battalion of English volunteers if its leaders knew how to go about it. Who would have guessed, twenty years ago, that the invention of the speedy motor-boat would have revived the half-forgotten adventure of smuggling,

or that the American Government would have intervened at that very moment with an unpopular pro-
hibition which, for the first time, made smuggling
pay?

Wireless telegraphy has greatly reduced the
dangers of shipwreck at sea. But when, long after
the War, the S.S. *Trevessa* foundered in the Indian
Ocean and there were no rescue ships at hand, her
captain and the crew took to their boats and, on an
unsatisfying diet of a little condensed milk, biscuits
and water, made a magnificent voyage of 1700 miles
to the Mauritius, almost equalling even Bligh's great
record. Captain Foster had been twice torpedoed
in the War, and had been one of a boat's crew of
thirty-one, of whom twelve died from exposure.
He used his previous knowledge well, and lost only
two native firemen from his own boat in the four
weeks' voyage, while the first officer in the other
boat, which was somewhat longer at sea, lost six
Indians and three Englishmen. Neither officer had
any trouble with his men. Both kept diaries, and the
following entry from the first officer's may serve as
an example of their delightfully cool and artless style:

June 11 (1923). Day begins with light wind.
Anyway we are moving, so that's something. I
am getting fed up with a rivet that is chafing my
hip when steering. Noon position, dead reckon-
ing, etc., etc.

No, the spirit is not dead. It has survived this post-
War unhappiness; it has survived the caricature of
itself made by the record-breaking craze and the

innumerable "publicity stunts," and it will survive all the stunt-makers. As long as the English race exists, there will be English adventurers. It is bred in the bone.

Seeking vainly for some kind of distinction between English adventurers and those of other nations (see Chapter I), I recently applied to one of the editors of this series for help. "What," I asked, "is the true distinction, if any, for I have been unable to find one, between English adventurers and the rest?" "There were more of them," he answered. And I think he uttered a great truth.

There were more of them. Not so much at any given period—though it would be easy to find such periods—but spread out over the whole. At one moment Italians have shown up in front, only to drop back again; at another Spaniards and Portuguese; at another Frenchmen and Dutch. Their colours show in front for a time, then disappear. But the English effort has never ceased. As a team, their score—if we add it up like the score of cross-country runners—must be easily the best, though an Englishman was not always the winner. We may not have staged the star turns, but we have ever been far behind.